PUBLISHED IN JUNE 1994

THE TITLE, STYLE OF MAKE-UP AND CONTENTS OF THIS
ALMANACK ARE STRICTLY COPYRIGHT

FOULSHAM'S
ORIGINAL MOORE'S
ALMANACK

1697   *THE ORIGINAL COPYRIGHT EDITION*   **1995**

1995: Year of Optimism

I foresee periods this year when the Nation enjoys waves of enthusiasm and my keynote for the year is *excited optimism*. 1995 will reveal signs of change in our thinking. Attitudes and values will be tested with surprising results. Even our prejudices will be affected by an ongoing mood-swing which starts this year.

On January 16th Pluto enters Sagittarius, a philosophical, far-seeing and adventurous sign. I expect it to herald a change in political thinking and to produce a stronger, idealistic view of politics. In Britain this radical shift will be towards the centre. I expect *condensed,* centred politics to emerge with almost no room for the traditional Left or Right of the spectrum. This may be less apparent during the Spring period, but should be very clear later on. It will then become increasingly difficult to understand the difference between one political party and another. Across the parties their leaders will speak as if they were of the same opinion. And Britain will begin a move towards the politics of *dynamic liberalism —* somewhat light on discipline.

Ideas or expressions of peace and universal brotherhood will flourish under these prevailing trends. We must be aware however, that such lofty expressions may conceal a hidden agenda. The danger will be that those who have been active in the politics of Terrorism or even organised Benefits Fraud will see our national mood as weakness and try to play upon it further. People of goodwill should be genuinely excited by the new start which 1995 offers. It represents a period when the Nation can produce the balance between self-reliance and an acceptance that the weak must not suffer.

© **1994 by W. FOULSHAM & CO. LTD.**   **Tel. SLOUGH (0753) 526769**
Printed in England by Benham & Co., Colchester.

In economic terms we will continue to feel an easement. Where 1994 offered *periods* of more growth in spending, this year will be much more even. It will provide a steady growth in the circulation of money and Business will at last begin to believe that fear is now part of its history.

There will be pressure on Britain to contribute ever more to NATO, the United Nations and others. We are increasingly likely to say No and to adopt a more *European* view of our role. In part this will weaken our "Special relationship" with the U.S.A.

Whereas in the past we have had to deal only with the problems of international politics, 1995 will bring us new problems from international criminals. Throughout Europe in particular borders have been relaxed. The Common Market will be seen to be very vulnerable to careful, masterful strategies, which export new criminal activities to new markets.

In Eastern Europe, particularly, I expect a strong leaning towards the old and even ancient ways. Communism will be voted back to live alongside the Capitalism of neighbouring States. While elsewhere, the traditional struggles of partisan, ethnic and religious groups will often ignite into warfare. In this context the worlds' peace keeping forces will be stretched beyond their capability and where Britain is no longer prepared to play an *active* role, our Diplomats are likely to be very involved in wise and fruitful diplomacy.

A noticeable feature around the world will be the significant rise in religious fervour and spirituality. Beyond the shores of our somewhat conservative Britain, I am expecting to see mass spirituality and some great excitement about the prospect of a Second Coming. This will be a year in which to expect an increasing number of self-proclaimed Prophets and Messiahs. Even in Britain I expect to read regular news stories about happenings which embody way-out beliefs.

In world terms too we will learn more of Dictators, their aggression and their plans. This is the kind of news which will be the legacy of 1995; To learn is to oppose and impair. Such repressive systems will find it difficult to survive in the climate of international, democratic, goodwill which is at the core of the influences this year. Even our own civil service will face pressures for less secrecy as the year unfolds.

The Tarot Trump for 1995 is 6 (i.e. $1 + 9 + 9 + 5 = 24; 2 + 4 = 6$) and represents the fork of two paths. This indicates that the world must make its choice for onward direction. On the one hand uncontrolled *freedom to excess* and on the other *disciplined reason*. The astrological aspects at this time show that Pluto enters Sagittarius and Uranus enters Aquarius. Thereby we have our answer whatever the rest of the world decides; controlled reason is the way forward for Britain. *Excessive* optimism and *misplaced* enthusiasm must be curbed during what should otherwise be a much more relaxed year for us all.

Old Moore extends his best wishes to all readers for a peaceful and prosperous year ahead.

Old Moore December 1993

Please name FOULSHAM'S ALMANACK when replying to Advertisers

Your Personal Horoscope from EQUINOX

*B*y unlocking the secrets contained in your Astrological Birth Chart you will gain a new and personal power over your destiny. Discover yourself through the pattern of the Universe and plan your future with greater confidence. Your Equinox Horoscope can enrich and even change the course of your life.

A. CHARACTER PORTRAIT. *A full interpretation of your Birth Chart. Identifies the real you, how others see you, reveals your individual path to social, romantic, spiritual and material success as well as other deeper hidden strengths within you.* **15 pages £14**

B. CHILD PROFILE *gives parents additional insight into their child's potential talents and future prospects in terms of education and career through insight into the planetary influences at the moment of birth.* **14 pages £14**

C. YEARLY FORECAST *offers the key to your future. Tells you when you'll be on top form and helps you to understand your changing moods by identifying the cycles of the planets in your chart now and over the next twelve months.* **10–20 pages £16**

D. THE COMBINATION *of both the Character Portrait and Yearly Forecast* **25–35 pages £25**

E. COMPATIBILITY PROFILE *explores the potential for a loving relationship between you and your partner. Besides the central theme of love and emotional intimacy, it helps you to understand and improve the quality of a close union by comparing both individual horoscopes.* **£20**

Each chart is a unique document.
The data for the Rising Sign, the planets and the aspects are calculated by computer and the interpretation is written by leading astrologer, Robert Currey.

Equinox
78 Neal Street
London WC2H 9PA
071-497 1001

Personal Horoscope

To receive your Equinox Horoscope within ten days, simply complete, cut out or photocopy this form and send it, together with your cheque/postal order, to EQUINOX (OM5) 78 Neal Street, London WC2H 9PA

TITLE MR/MRS ETC	INITIALS	LAST NAME		

Urgent Orders: Telephone (071) 497 1001 during office hours with the birth details and pay by Credit Card. Urgent Orders are subject to £1 post and handling charge.

ADDRESS · PLEASE PRINT

POSTCODE

* Time of Birth. If you don't know your time of birth, a special, though less extensive 'Flat' chart can be drawn up.

FIRST NAME	LAST NAME	SEX M OR F	BIRTH DATE DAY MONTH YEAR	* BIRTH TIME HOURS/MINUTES	PLACE OF BIRTH IF SMALL PLACE ADD NEAREST TOWN	CIRCLE CHARTS REQUIRED	TOTAL £
				AM/PM		A B C D E	
				AM/PM		A B C D E	

EQUINOX (OM5) 78 Neal Street, London WC2H 9PA   Orders by post include post and packing   Grand Total £

WORLD AFFAIRS — A Prophetic Preview

WORLD PROPHETIC PREVIEW

The period around the start of 1995 is likely to see a deepening of the belief in collective welfare, away from the old Thatcher and Reagan era of individual reliance. We should find therefore that socialist movements recover some of the confidence and even militancy that may have been lost in recent years.

UNITED KINGDOM

It would be unwise to consider any of the major British party leaders secure, immediately prior to or during the year of 1995. All political factions are regrouping, either in the knowledge of a rapidly changing view of politics by the electorate, or as a result of circumstance. To this end, it is highly likely that liberal forces are at work, making he demarcation between Left and Right more murky than ever. Watch for the rising fortunes of Paddy Ashdown and the Liberal Democrats as a result. And look for significant attacks in his direction from other areas of Westminster. John Major's fortunes are at best variable.

A snap election is not out of the question this year, with February and March being the most likely months, June and November the third and fourth options. Astrological trends are so finely balanced, that a resounding victory for any party would be less than likely. There will also be considerable pressure for home-rule in Scotland as mainstream politicians accept the nationalist agenda. We can expect substantial constitutional experiments in Northern Ireland. Although considerable doubts remain, the chance for peace is better this year than at any time since the troubles began. However, extremism is not dead in the Province and some residue of violence will be perpetuated.

Arguments are likely to abound between the Government and the BBC. This could lead to a complete restructuring of the Corporation and in turn to a significant redistribution of media personalities to independent broadcasters before July. Thanks to British research, there could be a leap forward in the medical treatment, both of cancer and also possibly AIDS.

THE BRITISH ROYAL FAMILY

There are efforts afoot during 1995, probably unsuccessful, to change the nature of Britain's constitution. These efforts should be strong enough to see the Monarchy in the news regularly. The Queen herself may keep a slightly lower profile, whilst other members of her family, most notably the Princes Andrew and Edward, are both supplying news fairly early in the year that will positively lift the profile of the Royal Family. Definite signs of conflict within the Royal household appear on two fronts: the first being associated with religious observance and its relationship to the Monarchy; the second regarding further revelations associated with past events in the lives of the Prince and Princess of Wales. A dark interlude may overshadow other royal reports around November. Despite these slight reversals, 1995 looks to be the best year for the Royals for some time.

POLITICAL EXTREMISM

A general warning must be sounded. Under the first signs of the coming idealistic surge prompted by Pluto's entry into Sagittarius and Uranus' entry into Aquarius, political ideas will begin to lose touch with reality. Under such circumstances the prospects are good for charismatic leaders such as Russia's nationalist leader, Zhironovsky, and/or others as yet unknown in the Middle East. To regard such leaders as a joke, or to write off their support as no more than a protest vote would be a serious mistake.

THE WORLD ECONOMY

It is increasingly difficult to talk about a single world economy, especially now that European and American financial muscle is being challenged by China, Japan and the other states of the western Pacific Rim. The western world will have pulled out of the deep recession which began in 1989. Economic confidence, world-wide, will continue to build. However, the share index position remains uncertain. Indeed, the economic situation will be finely balanced and market fluctuations will be more susceptible than usual to the daily news.

THE UNITED STATES

The USA will be in an expansive and assertive mood, bursting with renewed confidence. We should expect a major new statement of foreign policy doctrine around January or February, with naval or military engagements overseas in July or November.

RUSSIA

Although there is no respite from power struggles in Russia, the prospect of total collapse is not evident in 1995. The country is likely to be in an expansive mood and the power of the central government will be reinforced as the government moves towards a system of elected Czars. In March and April the country could be on military alert, and a coup, or some other military action can be expected around mid-month. The communists are likely to be gaining in support.

CHINA

The most important development in China could be a slowing in economic growth. Contraction may be necessary in order to stop economy 'overheating'. In addition, the influence of the old revolutionary leaders should now be over, and the government will consist of technocrats who never experienced the guerilla struggles. China enters the year under a prolonged Mars alignment, which is strongest from mid-February to mid-March and represents a classic war indicator. The British government should be warned.

THE MIDDLE EAST

The threat which radical Islam has posed to the Israeli peace process is diminishing; although the dream of an Islamic world will still be a powerful motivating factor. In particular, from May to August there will be revived fears of a nuclear war in the Middle East. I see the possibility of a political assassination in Egypt around mid-July. The Iraqi horoscope, set for August 23, 1921, shows long-term pressures in Iraq in May-August and November-December. There could be an attempt to assassinate the President in late May or mid-October.

New Breakthrough In Brain/Mind Research
to create who and what you want to be

– – – NO RISK ORDER FORM – – –
ORDER 4, CHOOSE 1 FREE! £9.95 each
✓ *please tick your choices & post today*

RX101	Powerful Person Programming
RX102	Attracting Perfect Love
RX103	A Calm & Peaceful Mind
RX104	The Good Life — Health, Wealth & Happiness
RX105	Accelerated Learning
RX106	Dream Solutions
RX107	Success & Excellence
RX108	Your Last Cigarette
RX109	Take Control of Your Life
RX110	Satisfaction & Happiness
RX111	Perfect Weight, Perfect Body
RX112	Sleep Like A Baby
RX113	The Upper Hand — Quick Thinking
RX114	Become A New Person
RX115	Create Wealth
RX116	Radiant Health
RX117	Healing Force
RX118	Right Brain Solutions
RX119	Feel Secure Now
RX120	Successful Independent Lifestyle
RX121	Banish Pain
RX122	Love Myself — Self-Esteem
RX123	Speak up — Say what you want to say
RX124	Weight Loss
RX125	How To Decide Exactly What You Want
RX126	Concentration Power Plus
RX127	Incredible Self-Confidence
RX128	Intensify Creative Ability
RX129	The Power of Persistence
RX130	Tennis
RX131	A Great Memory
RX132	Power & Success
RX133	Speed Reading
RX134	Charisma
RX135	Do More in Less Time
RX136	Ultimate Relaxation

£	Sub Total = Tapes × £9.95 each	
£1.95	Handling & Delivery	
£	TOTAL	

Please rush me my selections. I enclose
☐ CHEQUE ☐ POSTAL ORDER
payable to NEW WORLD CASSETTES
or charge my ☐ ACCESS ☐ VISA

☐ **YES** PLEASE SEND ME WITHOUT OBLIGATION, YOUR FULLY ILLUSTRATED FREE CATALOGUE OF OVER 250 FINE RECORDINGS

MR/MRS/MISS _____

ADDRESS _____

_____

_____ POST CODE _____

POST TO: **OM5**

NEW WORLD CASSETTES, PARADISE FARM
WESTHALL, HALESWORTH, SUFFOLK IP19 8RH
Instant Telephone Ordering Service for
ACCESS/VISA Card Holders

Access **0986-781-682** *VISA*

Incredible Self-Confidence
A Dick Sutphen
RX17 Digital-Holophonic™ Audio Cassette
The Most Powerful Brain/Mind Programming Tape In The World

Weight Loss
A Dick Sutphen
RX17 Digital-Holophonic™ Audio Cassette
The Most Powerful Brain/Mind Programming Tape In The World

A Calm & Peaceful Mind
A Dick Sutphen
RX17 Digital-Holophonic™ Audio Cassette
The Most Powerful Brain/Mind Programming Tape In The World

Your Last Cigarette No Exceptions!
A Dick Sutphen
RX17 Digital-Holophonic™ Audio Cassette
The Most Powerful Brain/Mind Programming Tape In The World

THE MOST POWERFUL BRAIN/MIND PROGRAMMING IN THE WORLD

RX17 Digital-Holophonic™ Audio Cassette Tapes introduce a new breakthrough in self-change programming. They incorporate state-of-the-art digital recording and the latest brain/mind technology to synchronize both halves of your brain. You are then receptive to new programming to change your beliefs and circumstances.

These are the most powerful audio programming tapes in the world. You don't even have to believe they will work in order for them to be effective. When properly accessed, your brain will accept new suggestions as reality. As an additional benefit, no matter what **RX17** program you use, you'll experience a great reduction in stress. Use Side A once a day and Side B as often as you want. You'll soon start to see the results. All it takes is the self-discipline to keep using the tape.

RX17 tapes are a product of the most advanced level of sound technology. We guarantee that you will immediately hear the difference — in quality, content and effectiveness. Each **RX17** tape is one hour long on Chrome Cassette and is packaged in a beautiful, full colour, book size case with a slide-out inner tray, which holds the tape. The subliminal suggestions are printed on the back along with further information and instructions. **RX17** tapes are available for £9.95 each.

Thanks to new technology and contemporary awareness of how the mind works, change no longer has to be difficult

☆ ☆ ☆ SPECIAL OFFER ☆ ☆ ☆
Choose any 4 titles and select a 5th
ABSOLUTELY FREE!
OR ORDER 8 AND CHOOSE 2 FREE

GUARANTEE: ORDER WITHOUT RISK
All our products are unconditionally guaranteed.
If for any reason you are not 100% satisfied with any item you order from us, just return it within 21 days of receipt for an immediate replacement or refund.
DELIVERY: Your orders will normally be despatched within 48 hours of our receiving them, but please allow 14 days for delivery.

FREE CATALOGUE
OF OVER 250 FINE RECORDINGS

New World Cassettes has over 100,000 satisfied customers and is the largest U.K. producer of both Self-Help cassettes and a unique selection of relaxing New Age Music. Their fully illustrated colour catalogue features over 250 of the finest recordings from around the world — on Chrome Cassette, Compact Disc and on Video. Send or phone for your free catalogue today.

VISIT OUR UNIQUE SHOP
An Aladdin's Cave of Crystals, Crafted Jewellery and Art of Myth and Legend, and hundreds of Recordings (including all the RX17s) at:
NEW WORLD AURORA, 16a Neal's Yard
Covent Garden, London WC2

DICK SUTPHEN

Each advancement in self-change mind programming has come from researcher and author Dick Sutphen. He has spent 21 years researching and teaching human potential awareness, and now medical practitioners attend his professional training programme to incorporate his life-changing techniques into their own practices.

Dick Sutphen was the first to create and market hypnosis tapes in 1976, and today he presents the **RX17 Audio Series** — the ultimate in brain/mind technology combined with state-of-the-art **Digital** and **Holophonic** recording technology.

NEW WORLD CASSETTES, PARADISE FARM, WESTHALL, HALESWORTH, SUFFOLK IP19 8RH. TEL: 0986-781-68

MICHAEL BARRYMORE

Michael was born 4 May 1952 in Bermondsey, London, at 8 am which makes him a hard-working Sun Taurus with Moon in modest, methodical Virgo. As for Michael's rising sign, he was born right on the cusp between late Gemini and early Cancer. Both signs influence his personality—Gemini gives versatility, quick responses, and talkativeness; Cancer bestows warmth and emotional sensitivity. Whichever sign one votes as the strongest, Uranus—the planet of originality and independence—is in his first house, making him a master of anarchy and giving him his unique brand of comedy inventiveness and serendipity.

Taurus–Virgo is a very earthy combination, giving charm, poise, a practical turn of mind, and an appreciation of material security. His bawdy, comfy sense of humour is instinctive. Taureans are also long on diligence, and this is true in Michael's case as he served many years' apprenticeship before his rise to mega-popularity. With Jupiter in Taurus as well, Michael's ideals are pragmatic and obtainable. Sun and Jupiter in Taurus bestow a deep contentment with himself and the capacity for enjoying the simple pleasures and ironies of life. This innate confidence attracts affection and that enviable quality of "luck". The Taurean trait of not giving up easily is even more extreme in his chart due to a Sun/Jupiter-Mars opposition. There is something in his nature which constantly seeks challenge, which *has* to win. The cheeky glint in his eyes comes from the exhilaration of the chase; Mars in Scorpio is relentless, but gives a terrific creative energy and a tendency to over-do. Not short of drive and commitment, Michael himself says he wishes he knew how to turn off the adrenalin once the show is over. A bout of extreme nervous exhaustion propelled him into therapy where he has had to face the self-destructive side of excessive creative energy.

Michael's horoscope contains three oppositions, all centred around the houses of the chart to do with self-expression and "show-biz". This indicates a high degree of creative tension, and a need to seek a balance between public and private life. A very close Mercury–Neptune opposition, in wide square to eccentric Uranus, reveals a vivid imagination and heightened mental perceptiveness, with great swiftness and accuracy of insight. This is the mark of mental originality and slick verbal repartee, but also a sign of mental over-sensitivity and a proneness to confuse outer reality with inner fantasy. Saturn and Neptune in his 5th house indicate the desire to be loved and the terrific pressure to achieve which drives him and creates more stress than he can handle. It also shows that there is a little kid inside him whose trapped miserable feelings can still debilitate and bewilder.

A warm, gregarious, fun-loving Venus–Jupiter conjunction symbolises his ease with people and love of the limelight, but a much more humble, home-loving side is shown by his Virgoan Moon. This is the domestic and 'ordinary' Michael which is nurtured by cooking, looking after his pet dog, and being looked after by his capable manager-wife. This is also the personable, approachable Michael who can talk to people with real interest, concern, and discreet playfulness. His Virgoan lunar side prefers a quiet, orderly life and finds all the razzamatazz of success a bit overwhelming. He is discriminating and perfectionist when it comes to his work, but is very sensitive to criticism from others.

Throughout 1995 Jupiter's benevolent influence affects his 6th house of work and health, lending support to the healing and strengthening of Michael's mind/body/soul. But with Saturn sojourning through his 10th house and opposing his Moon, he will need to keep a firm balance between honouring emotional needs and career opportunities. Favourable progressions of Venus and Jupiter reveal his success and popularity is a sure thing for many years to come.

Your 1995 Birthday
YOUR PERSONAL FORTUNE AND GUIDE

One of the following monthly readings is **PERSONAL TO YOU. Good days for Romance, Business, Finance, Travel and Social Affairs.** Each monthly forecast gives both your general and actual Birthday fortune for 1995 as well as

YOUR PLANETS, BIRTHSTONE AND YOUR LUCKY DAY

 ## CAPRICORN BORN PEOPLE

Birthdays between December 22nd and January 20th inclusive. Your planet is Saturn. Birthstone, garnet. Lucky day, Saturday.

KEYNOTE FOR THE YEAR   You have tremendous resources at your disposal and should use them to the full during 1995. Practical matters go especially well in the middle of the year.

JANUARY   INFLUENCES: 1-2nd An energetic and enterprising start to the year with plenty to set it apart. 12-13th Confidence may not be too high but others are willing to help. 25-26th Messages come from a host of different directions, keep your eye on the post. OPPORTUNITIES: 15-17th A better time financially, and one in which lady luck is on your side. LIMITING INFLUENCES: 28-29th Not everyone is equally helpful and you would be well advised to stick mainly to those you know well.

FEBRUARY   INFLUENCES: 1-2nd Doing what you want and what you know to be right may not be the same thing at all just at present. 13-14th A new and interesting social phase now opens up for you. 22-23rd The attitude of your best friends is somewhat difficult to understand, so patience is required. OPPORTUNITIES: 10-11th An enterprising period when it comes to dealing with any financial matter. LIMITING INFLUENCES: 27-28th Confronting past issues that were difficult could prove to be no less easy now.

MARCH   INFLUENCES: 2-3rd Give yourself the time you need to assess situations before you become involved in them. 16-17th A complete change of scenery would do you the world of good if only you could find the time. 24-25th Probably the most busy part of the month, though nonetheless useful for that fact. A time to keep trying. OPPORTUNITIES: 12-13th Better fortune follows your efforts, and especially so in terms of acquired wealth. LIMITING INFLUENCES: 27-28th Someone is trying to be difficult—and succeeding.

APRIL   INFLUENCES: 1-2nd Relationships prove awkward and this is not a good time for seeking an argument. 14-15th Confidence can be knocked for six, though only for a comparatively short time. 27-28th Strangely for Capricorn you have a real desire for adventure and change in your life during this period. OPPORTUNITIES: 21-22nd Coping with a number of different jobs, and all at the same time, is no real hardship. LIMITING INFLUENCES: 24-25th A large dose of optimism is called for at this time, but is not easy to come by.

CAPRICORN BORN PEOPLE

MAY INFLUENCES: 3-4th It's time for a change of scene, especially once work is out of the way. 17-18th Measure your successes against past efforts because you may be surprised at how far you have come recently. 27-28th A unique time and one that means surviving on your own initiative. OPPORTUNITIES: 21-22nd With plenty of drive, you push forward in several directions at once. LIMITING INFLUENCES: 15-16th Allow yourself the chance to take a rest, which may be badly needed at present.

JUNE INFLUENCES: 1-2nd The start of the month brings its own problems, even if few of them last very long. 12-13th Keeping an open mind is not too easy, especially with wayward relatives, some of whom may behave badly. 26-27th Life throws some surprising situations into your path and you will want to make the most of them. OPPORTUNITIES: 21-22nd With good luck more or less assured, you can afford to take the odd chance. LIMITING INFLUENCES: 15-17th The time to act is here, but do you have the energy necessary?

JULY INFLUENCES: 1-2nd You can't do everything yourself and you could find out that it is a mistake to even try. 14-15th There are certain people around who, try as you may, you just cannot get on with. 26-27th Confidence is on the increase again and you are very supportive of your best friends. OPPORTUNITIES: 23-24th Some useful pointers are around, especially in a personal sense, take note of them. LIMITING INFLUENCES: 9-10th Not everyone behaves quite as you might expect and some flexibility is necessary.

AUGUST INFLUENCES: 2-3rd A unique opportunity comes along to feather your own nest in ways you might never had dreamed of. 8-9th An early start and plenty of effort on both these days pays handsome dividends. 24-25th You realise that you may not have quite the influence over certain other people that you thought. OPPORTUNITIES: 14-16th A happy and interesting time, with great support coming in from outside. LIMITING INFLUENCES: 27-28th Realising your limitations is the lesson for now, and it isn't easy.

SEPTEMBER INFLUENCES: 1-2nd Not a period for beating about the bush when it comes to dealing with people in your vicinity. 14-15th A message is coming in from someone important—but are you listening carefully? 29-30th Not everyone has your best interests at heart, so look after your own life. OPPORTUNITIES: 21-22nd Look after the less well off and you find rewards coming back in your direction. LIMITING INFLUENCES: 17-18th You may be too studious for your own good and you do need variety.

OCTOBER INFLUENCES: 2-3rd Life is not quite what you would expect, but there is help about if you look for it. 15-16th A new and interesting social phase is about to open up for you. 19-21st Use your much improved powers of communication in order to explain a bright idea. OPPORTUNITIES: 25-26th Although you do not do it deliberately, you tend to gain from the losses of others at present. LIMITING INFLUENCES: 29-30th There just is not enough time to do all that you would wish.

NOVEMBER INFLUENCES: 3-4th Confronting issues that you do not care for the look of is a must as the month really gets started. 12-13th A veritable feast of delights socially awaits you now, though some effort is required too. 27-28th You have a heart of gold and the fact is all too obvious at present. OPPORTUNITIES: 17-18th There are some unique offers around for the taking and all you need to succeed is initiative. LIMITING INFLUENCES: 29-30th Not everyone is receptive to your ideas and talking them round is not easy.

DECEMBER INFLUENCES: 1-2nd Life puts you in a greater position of power than it has done for quite some time past. 16-17th A new and interesting phase begins to open up for you, particularly at work. 28-29th Plan year end functions in as much detail as you are able. OPPORTUNITIES: 24-25th The chance to enjoy an interesting and different sort of Christmas is there for the taking. LIMITING INFLUENCES: 12-13th People have the odd axe to grind with you, though of course, you don't have to join in.

Please name FOULSHAM'S ALMANACK when replying to Advertisers

LOWENDER

THE **GENUINE** LUCKY CORNISH PISKEY

For your good fortune and happiness

Everyone needs a little help sometime in their life. Now is your chance to get the help you need. ***MONEY – LOVE – HAPPINESS,*** whatever you dream of, the silver piskey from Cornwall could make your dearest wish come true.

By ancient tradition, the piskey's from Cornwall have helped people to find their way in life and to find the path that leads to good fortune and happiness.

LOWENDER, The piskey can put you on that path to good fortune. He has done it for others, let him do it for **YOU now.**

HAND CRAFTED ESPECIALLY FOR YOU, IN REAL SILVER. HAND ENGRAVED WITH THE ANCIENT CELTIC WORDS TO BRING YOU "PROSPERITY – HEALTH – HAPPINESS", AND WASHED IN THE MYSTERIOUS "POOL OF DOZMARY" ON BODMIN MOOR – HOME OF THE LUCKY CORNISH PISKEY.

MY GUARANTEE TO YOU — that every piskey will be made of solid silver. That your personal piskey will be washed in the "Pool of Dozmary" on Bodmin Moor and that every piskey will be signed on the reverse by "Merman" — only then will you know that your piskey is made with love and care by "Merman".

Remember — you owe it to yourself to have a **genuine** Cornish piskey with the **ADDED VALUE** of real silver.

"FREE" 18" SILVER CHAIN OR PLATED KEY RING – YOU CHOOSE. Super Value to you. For only £10.00 you will receive your own real silver Cornish piskey to carry with you for always. . . . ORDER NOW . . . Print you name and address on the coupon below. Enclose just £10.00 and post to "MERMAN".

- -

YES PLEASE — SEND MY LUCKY CORNISH PISKEY NOW. POST TO ADDRESS BELOW.
I ENCLOSE MY CHEQUE/P.O. FOR £10.00 MADE PAYABLE TO "MERMAN".

PLEASE PRINT   PLEASE TICK YOUR OWN CHOICE
NAME ....
                            18" CHAIN

ADDRESS ....
                            ☐
....
                            KEY RING

.... POSTCODE ....
                            ☐

POST TO: **Merman (O.P.), 1 Doneley Court, Berrycombe Road, Bodmin, Cornwall PL31 2NX**

AQUARIUS BORN PEOPLE

Birthdays between January 21st and February 19th inclusive. Your planet is Uranus. Birthstone, amethyst. Lucky day, Saturday.

KEYNOTE FOR THE YEAR Act with care early in the year, especially concerning your associations with others. Not everyone has your best interests at heart, though you are shrewd and well able to make all kinds of gains.

JANUARY INFLUENCES: 1-2nd Not a bad start to the year but don't expect to have everything all your own way. 15-16th Comfort and security seem to be on your mind more than usual right now. 27-28th A sudden reversal in trends works to your advantage, but some attention to detail is necessary. OPPORTUNITIES: 18-19th Keeping to a tried and tested path is not hard, even if you have to persuade others to do so too. LIMITING INFLUENCES: 30-31st It doesn't matter what you do, those around you seem determined to be difficult.

FEBRUARY INFLUENCES: 1-2nd A useful period, but not as exciting at first as you might wish. 14-15th An unusual period, during which help comes from unexpected directions. 27-28th Chickens from the past are inclined to come home to roost at this time. OPPORTUNITIES: 19-20th A careful review of past efforts could be invaluable in terms of your future plans. LIMITING INFLUENCES: 9-10th Don't expect people to rally round and help you as much as you might wish, at least for the next couple of days or so.

MARCH INFLUENCES: 2-3rd The arrival of March brings more in the way of personal choices into your life as a whole. 14-15th Not everyone is rooting for you now, though the most important people certainly are. 28-29th A unique chance to sort out something that has been on your mind for weeks or even months. OPPORTUNITIES: 21-22nd Few people would have the nerve to doubt or question your intentions at present. LIMITING INFLUENCES: 10-11th Material considerations will have to wait as money could be tight.

APRIL INFLUENCES: 1-2nd You are certainly no April fool as this month opens and your energy level is high. 15-16th Revisiting aspects of your past, you tend to look at them in new ways at present. 25-26th Unity and understanding are what you will be seeking personally at this stage of the month. OPPORTUNITIES: 19-20th Life offers some interesting challenges, most of which you will want to take up. LIMITING INFLUENCES: 27-28th Routines really are a drag and you should do all you can to avoid them.

MAY INFLUENCES: 1-2nd Along with the Spring comes a desire to make life more interesting and a need for excitement personally. 9-10th Aquarians of any age should feel at least young at heart during this interlude. 23-24th Some useful offers come along on the personal and professional fronts. OPPORTUNITIES: 15-16th Half way through the month, but certainly more than half the successes that you might expect coming along. LIMITING INFLUENCES: 26-27th Keeping your mind on the job in hand is not at all easy.

JUNE INFLUENCES: 2-3rd Active and enterprising, you can take the world by storm at this time. 13-14th Confidence takes a little knock, probably thanks to the actions of a friend. 21-22nd Prepare yourself for some sort of encounter which is difficult but useful. OPPORTUNITIES: 24-25th If you are prepared to keep confidences gains may well come along as a result. LIMITING INFLUENCES: 29-30th Slow and steady wins the race, and you cannot get much slower than these two days are likely to be!

JULY INFLUENCES: 1-2nd Don't put off until later the jobs that you know you should be doing right now. 12-13th A momentary lapse in concentration right now could prove to be difficult later on. 25-26th Someone has an offer which you will not want to refuse, even though you might realise that you should. OPPORTUNITIES: 19-20th Events confirm your suspicions that you are entering a much more dynamic period. LIMITING INFLUENCES: 29-30th The general atmosphere both at home and at work could be rather difficult.

Wash Away Your Worries

* **BRING BADLY NEEDED CASH – WITHIN 24 HOURS!**
* **BRING RELIEF FROM PAIN – WITHIN MINUTES!**
* **BRING SOMEONE TO LOVE YOU!**
* **BRING PROTECTION OF HOME & POSSESSIONS!**
* **BRING REJUVENATION OF BODY!**
* **BRING WINS AT BINGO & RACE TRACK!**
* **BRING PROTECTION FROM EVIL!**
* **BRING BACK A DISENCHANTED LOVER!**
* **BRING LUCK OVER AND OVER AGAIN!**

All Martha had to do was sprinkle her purse with water when she recited the special words in this book.

That very day Martha returned home with *three times as much in her purse* as when she left!

Jenny, cursed by chronic pain in her hip *experienced immediate relief after she performed the jug and water rite in this book!*

Sue, broken-hearted by her fiance's calling off their engagement, turned to the magic power of water, and that *very same day* he called begging her forgiveness! She performed the water rite again, and a month later they were married!

But why should so seemingly a foolish and superstitious faith in the power of water make such an impact?

Simply because water *is imbued with a spiritual and magical power which no other substance possesses.*

In drought people will kill each other for water. We cannot live without it. Two thirds of the human body is made up of it and almost three quarters of the earth's surface is under water.

Both religion and science – which can hardly agree on anything else – concede that life originated in water.

In the religious rites of every faith water is used as a purifier and as an agent for blessing and protection.

In the most ancient times people the world over believed in a Mother Goddess who came forth from the waters and created everything out of water.

In our Mother's womb we are immersed in her protective fluid.

Small wonder that subconsciously we hold water with such regard!

RESULTS WITHIN HOURS

Now both women and men can begin experiencing the *material benefits* of Water Magic, thanks to this amazing new book!

You could find your most pressing problems washed away within hours.

Jim from Atlanta was miraculously helped by Water Magic. He was only one hour away from being evicted from his home. With nothing left to lose he believed in the God-given power of water as he spoke the special words you will find in this book.

He was not turned out of his home.

Fortunately Mae from Tacome didn't face anything so serious. She enjoyed life's creature comforts, a nice home, and financial security. But she had no-one to share it with.

She performed the water rite on Monday. On Saturday the person of her dreams entered her life.

WHY THESE WATER RITES MUST WORK FOR YOU

Because water is so potent as a spiritual and magical metaphor it becomes irresistible. Mind power adepts speak of an *'Ocean of mind'*; the invisible universe is conceived in terms of fluid movement. We speak of the *thirst* for knowledge or power as if somehow these things that cannot be felt physically must therefore be liquid, that is – water.

We instinctively know its not nonsense to say 'bathed in luxury' or 'flooded with work'. An abundance of water suggests *an abundance of everything else.* Earth – physical density – is barren without rain.

You can now receive and enjoy all the things you desire by using the power that brings them – physical and metaphoric water!

You only need a jug or cup – and water! – to make this magic happen!

NOTHING COULD BE MORE NATURAL – OR POWERFUL!

SHE CAME TO ME

'I sought the company of the most beautiful woman in our corporation. So incredible were her looks that she seemed like Venus incarnate to me. But I honestly felt I didn't stand a chance with her.

'She knew me, but it was obvious that I was about as important to her as a fly on the wall. I couldn't even begin to summon the courage to ask her out. But I was crazy about her and I felt miserable.

'Then I learnt about the power of water and how it can affect women.

'It seemed as if I was dreaming when the very day after using the water rite *she asked me* for a date!

'It was then I became a believer.

'That happened just a few months ago and the lady in question is now my steady date!'

This extract from a testimonial from a Montreal man is strong proof of the power of water in matters of the heart!

WATER WORKS WONDERS!

Nothing could be easier than the water rites in this book.

You don't need paraphanalia of any kind.No witchcraft or mumbo jumbo.

Even a child can perform the rites in this book! They can be performed almost anywhere without atteacting the undesirable attention of others. And there is absolutely nothing in Water Magic that will compromise your religious beliefs.

You will be amazed at the results – results which can sometimes manifest within a few hours!

The uses of Water Magic are without end. Think of what you want, adapt the appropriate rite to your needs, and then wait for the result! Water Magic can bring you:

● WINS IN GAMES OF CHANCE, LOTTERIES, AND POOLS!
● THE LOVE AND ADMIRATION OF ANOTHER PERSON!
● RELIEF FROM HEALTH PROBLEMS! (Even cures have been reported!)
● A FLOOD OF ENDLESS RICHES INTO YOUR LIFE! (Perform Water Magic regularly to achieve this)
● STREAMS OF GOOD LUCK! (For making events *flow* to your advantage; let the tide of good fortune always be in your favour!)

Yes! Through the inexhaustable renewing power of *the very source of life itself* you can enjoy and ENDLESS FLOW OF GOOD FORTUNE!

Perform the water rites as often as you like to recieve everything you desire!

Persons from all walks of life are benefiting from the life-enriching powers of Water Magic! Read how:

WATER RITES HELP ANIMAL! – Pat C. was distressed by her cat's suffering. She sprinkled water on the painful area and the cat was immediately relieved!

WATER RITE BRINGS LOTTERY WIN – Kay W. won $10,000 after she slightly moistened her entry coupon with blessed water!

COLD LOVER PROPOSES SEX! Always indifferent to her sexual needs, June A. tried the power of water. She was astonished at the result!

KEEPS UNWANTED RELATIVES AWAY! – Ted G.'s relatives forever sponged on his good will. He had had enough of them so he sprinkled water outside his doorway making his wish – they never returned!

WATER RITE PREVENTS COLLISION! – A careful driver, Sally B. was always worried about the recklessness of other drivers. She 'blessed' her car with mystically charged water. When her car was completely untouched by two cars colliding only inches away from her she was convinced it was thanks to Water Magic!

WATER RITE MADE WEDDING BELLS RING! – Ann W. couldn't get her boyfriend to agree to a wedding date. She believed in the power of water, and the *very next day* he said he wanted marriage at the earliest possible date!

Now you can 'wash away your worries' and 'drink in' life's riches. With this book and nature's most precious commodity you cannot fail!

To order 'Water Magic' send £6.95 to:

**FINBARR (OW),
16 Turketel Road
Folkestone, Kent CT20 2PA**

Overseas send £9.20 to cover air mail. Catalogue of books 50p. Callers at this address only: 113 Dover Road, Folkestone.

We have advertised in Old Moore's since 1975.

AQUARIUS BORN PEOPLE

AUGUST INFLUENCES: 2-3rd A less constrained atmosphere at the beginning of the month brings a more enlightened attitude. 16-17th Acting on impulse is something to be avoided at this time. 23-24th Certain jobs are a little tedious, but you should get them out of the way as soon as possible. OPPORTUNITIES: 29-30th You can reach a better understanding with loved ones and should make gains as a result. LIMITING INFLUENCES: 18-19th Controlling your emotions is not easy but is really essential.

SEPTEMBER INFLUENCES: 2-3rd Act with certainty when you are dealing with subject matter that is close to your heart. 13-14th An eventful period, though perhaps not in quite the ways you might expect. 25-26th Stamina is in short supply so you will have to pace yourself a little. OPPORTUNITIES: 16-17th Even family arguments could be turned to your advantage, if you are clever in your approach. LIMITING INFLUENCES: 29-30th You tend to shun the sort of company that could be of the greatest importance to you, which could be a mistake.

OCTOBER INFLUENCES: 1-2nd Open the month with a flourish and show the world what you are capable of. 15-16th Not everyone has your best interests at heart, but you can bring them round given time. 22-23rd The general atmosphere around you is a little strained so do what you can to improve it. OPPORTUNITIES: 25-26th Do whatever you can to change direction in order to gain from improved financial possibilities generally. LIMITING INFLUENCES: 28-29th There is not enough time to do the things that appeal to you and work seems endless.

NOVEMBER INFLUENCES: 2-3rd There are tasks to perform that you don't like the look of. Get them out of the way early. 16-17th Realising your potential is easier now, but convincing others is less so. 24-25th Create space for yourself and don't be tied down by routines. OPPORTUNITIES: 12-13th Whatever your convictions are, you need to voice them now in order to achieve successes. LIMITING INFLUENCES: 29-30th The end of the month could prove to be a little dull unless you put in extra effort.

DECEMBER INFLUENCES: 1-2nd You already have Christmas in your sights and can plan well ahead. 16-17th Realism is not something that you really want to look at now and you tend to live in something of a dream world. 21-22nd Reversals are not long lasting and only have a minor part to play in your life. OPPORTUNITIES: 24-25th A very unusual and yet generally happy Christmas feeds your enthusiasm now. LIMITING INFLUENCES: 4-5th Not everyone is on your side, especially when it comes to new ideas.

PISCES BORN PEOPLE

Birthdays between February 20th and March 20th inclusive. Your planet is Neptune. Birthstone, bloodstone. Lucky day, Thursday.

KEYNOTE FOR THE YEAR   Not all the ideas that you bring from the past are of equal merit this year, and it turns out to be a mixture of the old and the new that brings the greatest success.

JANUARY INFLUENCES: 1-2nd Fruitful negotiations take place as the year opens, bringing the chance of some financial gain. 15-16th The attitude of loved ones might prove to be difficult to understand at some stage. 22-23rd Don't reproach yourself for situations that are not of your own making. OPPORTUNITIES: 17-18th There is plenty of incentive to get on in life, especially when it comes to financial gains. LIMITING INFLUENCES: 25-26th Recent stresses seem to get you down more than they really should.

NOW — JUST WHEN YOU NEED A REAL MONEY MIRACLE

RUB THE BUDDHA FOR MONEY!

RUB THE BUDDHA FOR MONEY!

Do you need money desperately? Are you up to your neck in overdue bills and worrisome debt? Are you struggling along just trying to make ends meet — with no light in sight?

Then, here's the good news you've been hoping and praying for all your life! Now for the very first time, you can possess the long-renowned BUDDHA acclaimed by many for its magic powers of attracting GREAT wealth and unbelievable riches to anyone who gently rubs his belly !

But before I go on let me ask you this: How much money do you really want? £100.00, £1,000.00, even £100,000.00 or more?

Don't be shy. Just name the amount. ANY amount. Then join me in a unique research experiment to find out if the BUDDHA legend is really true.

And listen to this, to make this offer so unbelievably attractive that you'll clip and mail the coupon right now, I'm going to gamble my own money on you, a perfect stranger.

Its good luck is guaranteed, or it won't cost you a single penny.

But first let me assure you of this. I know exactly what I'm doing. I wouldn't dare make such an offer if I thought for one minute that I would lose! So for your own sake, simply mail the coupon to receive your very own BUDDHA. Do you want lots of money NOW? Then starting immediately, and continuing for as long as you rub the BUDDHA, you'll have this sensational opportunity to possibly rub away your financial problems forever. Imagine the excitement and thrill of turning your cash situation RIGHT AROUND merely by rubbing The BUDDHA'S belly as part of the Experiment.

£££ When you want to pay off debts, simply rub The BUDDHA.

£££ When you want to go on a long-overdue vacation, simply rub The BUDDHA.

£££ When you want to buy a new car, TV, boat, or whatever you wish, simply rub The BUDDHA.

LET ME KNOW EVERY TIME THE BUDDHA BRINGS MONEY

Whenever The BUDDHA miraculously puts fist-loads of cash right into your pocket . . . Whenever you enjoy the glorious thrill of paying off a nagging bill collector . . . whenever you joyfully catch up on your monthly payments . . . just report the actual MONEY MIRACLE. Even if your are sceptical, you have absolutely nothing in the world to lose. Not even a penny of your hard-earned money. Because from the very moment you receive The BUDDHA, you must receive a fantastic money-blessing, or I'll refund your money.

And here is the best part of all! It doesn't matter who you are, where you live, how much you need! You MUST agree that the BUDDHA legend is true RIGHT AWAY, or I'll return your money.

SEND FOR YOUR BUDDHA AT ONCE WITHOUT RISK

Right now, this very second, mail the coupon for your very own BUDDHA. For total 100% confidentiality, your BUDDHA will be rushed back to you in a private unmarked package — in your name only. No one will be allowed to use it, except you. Then merely take The BUDDHA into your right hand and gently rub his magic belly. It's that simple!

I can't imagine anyone passing up this unique chance to join the Research Experiment and use the legendary BUDDHA every single day. If the only thing holding you back is taking a risk. I'm going to eliminate that completely!

To prove to you that I mean every word I've said — I'll give you this fantastic MONEY BACK GUARANTEE: The BUDDHA must work a money miracle for you, or I'll return your money.

If you've never thought of clipping a coupon before, do it NOW. It may be the answer to ALL your money problems.

ORDER RIGHT NOW FOR IMMEDIATE DELIVERY

1. Print your name and address on the coupon below.   2. Attach your cash, cheque or money order payable to: "Marie-Simone" for just £12 complete. (price includes postage and handling)! 3. mail to: "Marie-Simone," (Dept **OM95B**). Totteridge Village, London N20 8PN.

SEND £12,00 NOW!

"Marie-Simone", (Dept **OM95B**). Totteridge Village, London N20 8PN.

YES! By return mail rush me my magic BUDDHA on a 22" chain. Should the magic BUDDHA not work, I will return to you on the understanding you will return my £12.00.

I enclose cash/cheque/P.O. for £............
made payable to: "Marie-Simone".

Name............

Address ....

....

Date of Birth............

Reg No. 2079588

PISCES BORN PEOPLE

FEBRUARY INFLUENCES: 2-3rd Not everything you are looking for falls into your lap just at the moment. 9-10th Act with certainty and you can be fairly sure that others will come around to your point of view. 27-28th The end of the month has its own rewards, even if most of them are low-key. OPPORTUNITIES: 17-18th Vitality is high, allowing plenty of scope for getting things done practically. LIMITING INFLUENCES: 23-24th Making any sort of progress is going to be difficult at this stage and patience is necessary.

MARCH INFLUENCES: 1-2nd Reliance on friends could lead to its own form of disappointment at present. 13-14th Confidence is not at all high and you do need the support of some favoured individuals. 29-30th Your attitude towards professional matters is now very much better and so progress can be expected. OPPORTUNITIES: 22-23rd As long as you know that you are right, stick up for what you believe at all times now. LIMITING INFLUENCES: 25-26th Controlling your temper may not be too easy.

APRIL INFLUENCES: 2-3rd A revival of past ideas may seem interesting but turns out to be less important than you thought. 17-18th Keep an open mind about professional changes and don't turn down chances without looking at them. 25-26th A sudden reversal in one situation or another may well turn out to be to your advantage. OPPORTUNITIES: 12-13th Give some thought to what you want in a practical sense and put yourself to work getting it. LIMITING INFLUENCES: 27-28th There are some really awkward sorts of people to deal with now.

MAY INFLUENCES: 1-2nd You have a wealth of experience at your disposal and need to put it to work now. 12-13th A great surge of energy now comes your way, decide how best you should use it. 23-24th Confidence to do what you want is lacking, but can be assisted by the intervention of friends. OPPORTUNITES: 14-15th Very definitely a period for speaking your mind, even if others do not agree. LIMITING INFLUENCES: 27-28th Acting on impulse at this stage will only get you into trouble.

JUNE INFLUENCES: 1-2nd Not everyone appears to have your best interests at heart as the month opens, though they should soon come round. 14-16th Keep in touch with people who may be living at a distance from you. 24-25th A new and interesting social phase looks as though it is about to open up for you. OPPORTUNITIES: 20-21st Creating the right social atmosphere in order to enjoy yourself is easy. LIMITING INFLUENCES 5-6th Don't give in to pessimism.

JULY INFLUENCES: 2-3rd July brings all sorts of possibilities relating to travel and they start right now. 12-13th Convincing others that you know what you are talking about may not be all that easy. 24-25th You have plenty to say for yourself, that is if you can find anyone who will listen. OPPORTUNITIES: 16-17th A time to get yourself out and about, both socially and professionally. LIMITING INFLUENCES: 22-23rd Concentration is not easy to find, but essential if you want to succeed.

AUGUST INFLUENCES: 1-2nd Friends and relatives alike do all that they can to make your life easier as August opens. 17-18th Not a wonderful period, though good for doing what you know to be correct. 22-23rd Any ill health that may have been around now tends to abate somewhat. OPPORTUNITIES: 12-13th Creating a good atmosphere, either at work or at home is easy now. LIMITING INFLUENCES: 26-27th Comfort and security appeal to you, but are hard to find.

SEPTEMBER INFLUENCES: 2-3rd Not a remarkable start to the month, but probably quite lucky all the same. 9-10th Advantages come from some very surprising directions and some unusual people. 16-17th A new phase opens up with regard to your ability to succeed financially. OPPORTUNITES: 24-25th A steamy time romantically and one that offers much that is personally satisfying. LIMITING INFLUENCES: 29-30th The end of the month offers some tedious situations which you are going to find repressive.

Many said that his cards of ancient symbols were "magical, mystical and eternally powerful" and that anyone who owned them could help themselves to the great things in life they wanted. The late and great Dr. Joseph Ellah was known to many as a "miracle worker". Here is your chance to see his legacy to the world, the mystical and ancient symbols said to have touched the lives of all who came to see him.

THE CARDS OF DOCTOR ELLAH

Dr. Joseph Ellah collected together all of the most potent, fast-acting and successful symbols and designs from the wise men of the world, and by combining them together, he **created his own powerful design cards, known worldwide as THE CARDS OF DOCTOR ELLAH.**

These design cards with their incredibly 'powerful' and proven symbolism are said to have helped **thousands of people around the globe to find money, love, luck, good health, knowledge, learning and wisdom, success and respect, power and glory.**

THE CARDS OF DOCTOR ELLAH were the result of his life's work, and the reason it is said for his immense success in helping people to realise their dreams, improve their lives, and give them the things they needed quickly and effectively.

Doctor Ellah spent most of his life travelling around the world, teaching, healing, helping all who came to see him. He was allowed to meet gurus, yogis, tribesmen, men of mystery, witchdoctors, shamans, medicine men and magicians, indeed wise ones from all over the globe. He visited some of the remotest parts of the world, going to places where a white man had not been seen before, places where time had stood still, **he had access to the secret and mysterious knowledge of these people**, and he combined the most effective and fast-acting symbols being used **to create his own now famous 'CARDS OF DOCTOR ELLAH'.**

There are seven sets of cards, each for a different purpose in life, and there are twelve design cards to each set. (Doctor Ellah always used his cards in sets of twelve.) By showing these cards with their 'powerful' and mysterious symbols, Doctor Ellah is said to have helped countless thousands to find the things they wanted, 'quickly and effectively'.

NOW YOU CAN SEE FOR YOURSELF THE INCREDIBLE 'CARDS OF DOCTOR ELLAH'

DOCTOR ELLAH'S CARDS OF MONEY. Said to bring money, wealth, prosperity, riches, abundance, fine possessions, luxury, profits, freedom from debts and money worries, life-long financial security and financial independence. Also believed by some to help with the winning of money through all forms of gambling and investing or to help with the finding of money. *COMPLETE SET OF TWELVE MONEY CARDS ONLY £95.*

DOCTOR ELLAH'S CARDS OF LOVE. Said to bring IMMEDIATE love and romance, passion and pleasure, popularity and friendship, companionship or excitement, joy and happiness. Believed by some to make their owner more attractive, desirable, and irresistably beautiful. Used by men and women of all ages and from all backgrounds. Recognised universally as potent and 'successful' love bringers. *COMPLETE SET OF TWELVE LOVE CARDS ONLY £95.*

DOCTOR ELLAH'S CARDS OF LUCK. Said to bring an abundance of luck, good fortune, at all times and on all occasions, completely stopping all bad luck and misfortune, ending difficulties, frustrations and the bad luck which may have been holding you back, replacing these things with only good fortune, favourable circumstances, and incredibly good luck for ever more. *COMPLETE SET OF TWELVE LUCK CARDS ONLY £95.*

DOCTOR ELLAH'S CARDS OF GOOD HEALTH. Said to bring a full and speedy recovery from illnesses and even so-called incurable diseases or when conventional medicine has failed, help for all health problems, regardless of age or medical history, for complaints major and minor, large or small. Dr. Ellah is said to have proven the capabilities of these cards, and their "speed and effectiveness" on many occasions, and in many parts of the world. *COMPLETE SET OF TWELVE GOOD HEALTH CARDS ONLY £95.*

DOCTOR ELLAH'S CARDS OF KNOWLEDGE, LEARNING AND WISDOM. Said to bring unbeatable help in tests and examinations, ensuring clarity and accuracy in all that you say and write, making learning and understanding simpler, improving memory power, increasing intelligence and giving more sense and wisdom on all occasions. *COMPLETE SET OF TWELVE KNOWLEDGE, LEARNING AND WISDOM CARDS ONLY £95.*

DOCTOR ELLAH'S CARDS OF SUCCESS AND RESPECT. Said to bring success, respect, glory and confidence, make you unbeatable in all activities, and in all areas of life: home life, family life, business and career, love life, etc., and to ensure they recognise your success, respecting you and admiring you in the way you want. *COMPLETE SET OF TWELVE SUCCESS AND RESPECT CARDS ONLY £95.*

DOCTOR ELLAH'S CARDS OF POWER AND GLORY. Said to give you a power over others, make them listen to what you say, ensure that they act upon your advice and follow your wishes, giving you the power, glory, honour and prestige you deserve. (These cards are often used together with the Success and Respect cards mentioned above.) These Power and Glory cards together with the Success and Respect cards, are said to have been responsible for the power, glory and recognition given to kings, queens, princes and princesses, sheiks, rulers, presidents and leaders, statesmen, politicians, ambassadors, business magnates and tycoons from all around the world. *COMPLETE SET OF TWELVE POWER AND GLORY CARDS ONLY £95.*

'THE CARDS OF DOCTOR ELLAH' ONLY £95 PER SET OR ALL SEVEN SETS FOR £495

We are proud to be able to offer you these seven sets of cards, so that the marvellous knowledge gained by the late and great "miracle working" Dr. Joseph Ellah can continue. Each of these sets of cards contains twelve designs (Dr. Ellah always used them in sets of twelve, never individually.) These cards are faithful reproductions, passed on to us together with the ancient formulae used in their preparation. We will send these cards to you "fully prepared" to these traditional formulae. *May they help you as they seem to have helped thousands of others worldwide.*

Write down your name and address, tell us which of these sets of Doctor Ellah's cards you would like to own. Enclose payment by Postal Order or cheque (payable to 'CURIOCRAFT') and send your order to:

CURIOCRAFT (Dept. O), P.O. BOX 222, LINCOLN LN1 2RY, ENGLAND

PISCES BORN PEOPLE

OCTOBER INFLUENCES: 1-2nd Convincing yourself about anything is easier than trying to talk others round at this time. 16-17th Routines really can get you down so ring the changes. 25-26th A calmer and more rational period is now upon you. Try to enjoy yourself. OPPORTUNITIES: 12-13th Holding back is not for you at present, so do what you can to be yourself. LIMITING INFLUENCES: 18-19th A few people seem to be blocking your path to success. Try to ignore their presence.

NOVEMBER INFLUENCES: 1-2nd November brings certains doubts into your mind which should be dealt with early in the month. 23-24th Confidence is higher than for some time, make the most of passing chances. 29-30th Attitudes in your family are variable and you have to play the Devil's advocate. OPPORTUNITIES: 13-14th A greater degree of confidence in yourself cannot be a bad thing—use it! LIMITING INFLUENCES: 10-11th Not the best period for starting any sort of new venture or for sticking your neck out.

DECEMBER INFLUENCES: 1-2nd December opens with significant courage and enthusiasm on your part. 15-16th Planning the festive season could well be taking up most of your time now. 24-25th A new and interesting period coincides with the arrival of Christmas. OPPORTUNITIES: 11-12th Social highlights abound, bringing plenty of excuses for having a really good time. LIMITING INFLUENCES: 28-29th Convincing others that you know what you are talking about is not easy.

ARIES BORN PEOPLE

Birthdays between March 21st and April 20th inclusive. Your planet is Mars. Birthstone, diamond. Lucky day, Tuesday.

KEYNOTE FOR THE YEAR   Not everything you want is going to come your way immediately and some patience is necessary until the Spring. In a general sense, confidence for the year as a whole does tend to be high.

JANUARY INFLUENCES: 1-2nd A reasonable start to the year, with better financial planning possible. 12-13th New and positive attitudes develop where personal relationships are concerned. 27-28th Turn your mind in the direction of new possibilities for advancement at work. Romance is in the air. OPPORTUNITIES: 19-20th Give yourself more credit for successes and move forward positively. LIMITING INFLUENCES: 5-6th Not everyone is in the right mood to help you out at this time.

FEBRUARY INFLUENCES: 3-4th Compensations are necessary to balance finances, though money is available. Don't put off projects that you know are important. 16-17th Compliments come your way that feed you with greater enthusiasm. 26-27th A good time to travel, or at least for planning a journey. OPPORTUNITIES: 21-22nd Friends want to involve you in what could be money-making schemes. LIMITING INFLUENCES: 19th Trouble from the opposite sex could restrict your power to please yourself.

MARCH INFLUENCES: 2-3rd All your effort tends to be put into practical issues at present, but save time for rest. 10-11th A variable period, though social possibilities are better than business matters or even your personal life. 25-26th You are in a position to help people who are less well off than you. OPPORTUNITIES: 7-8th If you have been looking for a real bargain, this is the time to keep your eyes open. LIMITING INFLUENCES: 19-20th Lack of personal influence becomes a stumbling block now.

"I DON'T BELIEVE IT!!!"

Most people say that when someone tells them about the **Wishing
Cork Tree** and its 350-year-old
legend because it really is difficult
to believe. How can a piece of cork
affect their fortunes? It's ridiculous, why should it be so
lucky? It's all nonsense, I DON'T BELIEVE IT and so on
and so on. A wife gave her doubting husband a piece just
for fun and two weeks later he won £1,500. A lady from
Newark bought a piece and very soon after won £1,000
on the premium bonds. A gentleman from Flint was given
a piece when he was so ill that the doctors had given him
24 hours to live, believe it or not he started to get better
straight away. A couple from Peterborough wrote to say
that the day they bought their cork, over 20 years ago,
was the turning point in their lives and they have never
wanted since. A lady from Bristol won a colour television
within a week of receiving her cork. These are just a few
of the many letters received telling of bingo wins, new
houses, pools wins and good health. Royalty, Cabinet
ministers and film stars are amongst those who have had
a piece just for fun. Two of my family have won £6,000
and £3,000 respectively on the football pools so there
must be something in it.
If you would like a piece please send £1.50 (3 for £3.00,
8 for £5) and a <u>stamped addressed envelope</u> to:

IRIS FISHER
PO Box 113, Lincoln LN1 3HP

ARIES BORN PEOPLE

APRIL INFLUENCES: 6-7th Creative potential now makes you look at life in a very different way. 9-11th Go with the flow, but don't accept situations you don't like the look of. 29-30th Stick to your guns personally but try to remain reasonably flexible. OPPORTUNITIES: 14-15th More movement romantically makes for a good time and plenty of new incentives. LIMITING INFLUENCES: 18-19th Not the best time for trying to get your own way, since others are not approachable in the way that you would wish.

MAY INFLUENCES: 1-2nd Give yourself the chance to recover from past excesses before pushing yourself too hard. 12-13th Even casual conversations have something interesting to tell you, if you only choose to listen. 22-23rd Pride tends to be high, and you can easily influence the thinking of other people. OPPORTUNITIES: 15-16th A good time to stick with your principles, even if others do disagree. LIMITING INFLUENCES: 19-20th Partnerships of any sort are not advised at this time.

JUNE INFLUENCES: 1-2nd Half way through the year, but are you really trying as hard as you should practically? 10-11th A growing need to exercise your own rights professionally. 23-24th Give yourself a pat on the back when you know that you have achieved a personal coup. OPPORTUNTIIES: 14-15th The best time of the month for give and take, which both bring significant rewards. LIMITING INFLUENCES: 19-21st Confined in your own mind, you tend to push the world outside away, which is a mistake.

JULY INFLUENCES: 4-5th Standard responses do not work at this time, so set out to be original. 12-13th Creativity is very high, and remains so for a few days ahead. 27-28th New love comes into your life, though it could bring the odd problem to bear on you in terms of decision-making. OPPORTUNTIES: 7-8th Nobody can deny the giving quality of your nature now and the world tends to reply in kind. LIMITING INFLUENCES: 29-30th The need for security takes up too much of your time, restricting your movements.

AUGUST INFLUENCES: 3-4th Be as bold as you need to be in your desire to have things turn out specifically the way you would wish. 12-13th A particular situation personally needs careful handling, which you can easily supply. 25-26th Stick to your principles, since others are inclined to follow your lead. OPPORTUNITES: 16-17th Perhaps the best time of the month for looking out a bargain at the shops. LIMITING INFLUENCES: 18-19th Not enough enthusiasm for new projects, especially at home.

SEPTEMBER INFLUENCES: 2-3rd Emotional responses are good, and your ability to talk has rarely been better than now. 11-12th Personalities of one sort or another tend to enter your life now. 22-23rd Once you have decided on a course of action professionally, it is important to stick to it. OPPORTUNITIES: 15th The best day of the month to change attitudes in mid stream. LIMITING INFLUENCES: 9-10th Grasping at straws is worse now that deciding that in some ways you should be starting from scratch.

OCTOBER INFLUENCES: 2-3rd Someone you have been thinking about makes an entry into your life. 19-20th Confusion in personal relationships is avoided by your good powers of communication. 27-28th Out and about much more than has been possible recently, you make an excellent impression on just about everyone. OPPORTUNITIES: 5-6th Look out for changes in routines that definitely suit you. LIMITING INFLUENCES: 21-22nd Things may not turn out as you would wish when it comes to romantic attachments.

NOVEMBER INFLUENCES: 1-3rd Going with the flow is best, especially when you know that there is definitely some help around. 16-17th A really sympathetic Arian is able to offer support that is returned later. OPPORTUNITIES: 9-10th Wherever it proves to be possible, make the most of improving general good luck. LIMITING INFLUENCES: 28-29th Not everyone is responsibe to what you see as being flexibility.

DECEMBER INFLUENCES: 2-3rd Give and take are important at this time, but you might be doing most of the giving. 9-10th A slow and steady period, but probably a very happy one too. 22-23rd Routines could get you down unless you are willing to ring the changes and make life react in the way that you would wish. OPPORTUNITIES: 15-16th Even in the face of some opposition you have the power to put your point of view across forcefully. LIMITING INFLUENCES: 17-18th Creating the right impressions socially is something you find difficult to do right now.

SALT MAGICK WORKS — THESE UNSOLICITED TESTIMONIALS PROVE IT:

'Have already had two wins on the pools' — *M. B. (Fleetwood)*
'In ten minutes my voilent son quietened down after I did the salt rite . . . I've had no trouble from him since' — *P.E. (Manchester)*
'IT REALLY WORKS! . . . I won £1411' — *A.P. (Grimsby)*
'Since I got your book . . . money has come into my home in different ways . . . my son has paid off his debts . . . I bless the day I sent for this book' — *A.L. (Hove)* (This lady wrote again five months later: 'The salt is still working for us . . . every day we receive something good')
Photo-copies of these actual testimonials available on request. Many more available!

NEW SALT MAGICK RITES
BRING INCREDIBLE RESULTS . . . SOMETIMES WITHIN HOURS, EVEN MINUTES!

The average New Salt Magick Rite takes only minutes to do. And you can do it in the privacy of your own home.

All you need is common table salt and the wish to make your dreams come true.

NEVER HAS SALT MAGICK BEEN SO EASY. This brand new book show how anyone can do it. You only need a packet of salt — and (apart from this book) nothing else! **No other ingredients are required for most of the salt rites in this new book.**

You will be astonished at their simplicity — and even more astonished at the fast results!

SALT MAGICK WORKS. People have performed it for millinia to solve their problems.

Salt is incorruptible; and it is this quality which has given it a magickal significance in the minds of many people. It has always been used in magick ritual as a *repellent of evil forces.*

From time immemorial those acquainted with salt lore would dare not enter a new home *without first sprinkling salt outside the door.*

They *would not allow a new baby to leave home without carrying salt; nor would they swear oaths without the presence of salt.*

There are literally hundreds of salt superstitions. No other substance has generated so much magickal fascination. You will read of a few of these superstitions in this new book.

Perhaps the best known salt superstition is the dread of spilling salt, always believed to be a sign of impending disaster. The well known formula for averting disaster is to pick up the spilt salt and cast over the left shoulder. There is more about this in the book.

Did you know you could keep unwanted persons away from your home by sprinkling salt outside your door?

Read in this book what exactly it is you have to do.

In his foreward to Mr Pike's book writer Jim Barry explains how using salt in this way have kept unwanted persons out of sight. 'They have never troubled me again', he writes.

SALT MAGICK RITES WORK — AND THEY ARE PROVEN TIME AND AGAIN!

Sprinkle salt on pools and lottery coupons. Carry a pinch of salt when you go to place a bet.

Salt rites are easy, clean, and so simple to perform!

Anyone of any religious faith can do them!

TO PROTECT YOURSELF FROM BAD LUCK USE THESE SIMPLE NEW SALT RITES.

You will be astounded at the change in your life!

This brand new book shows how to get results . . . ove and over again! These simple rites *have never before been made public!* These are far simpler than the only other salt rituals previously published (in Marcus Bottomley's 'Salt Power' book, now out of print).

Jason Pike, the author of this new book has presented these Salt Magick Rites in such a way that even a child can perform!

The magic use of salt is of great antiquity but the new rites in this book are *made simple for today's busy woman and man!*

Mr Pike's own marriage was saved from divorce, thanks to Salt Magick! He writes, 'The end was at hand — we just couldn't live together any longer. I tried the salt rite in desperation . . . IT WORKED IMMEDIATELY! The peace that entered our home was unbelievable!

'Now we are happier than ever before!'

In this book you will find *the precise New Salt Magick Rite that saved his marriage.* It takes only minutes to do — and yet what wonders it can bring! You will find in this book:

● **New Salt Magick Brings Money.** See in Chapter 1 how it can solve your money worries! Receive cash from unexpected sources!

● **Command Another Person's Thoughts And Actions!** This seems unbelievable — but see Chapter 12! (Important: this cannot be used to *harm* someone. Salt Magick cannot be used is this way).

● **New Salt Magick For Regaining Youth.** This is an age-old formula. Those who have used it swear it works! But it takes 14 days to see results.

● **New Salt Magick For Protection.** Protect yourself and loved ones from physical injury!

● **Salt Rite To Get A Job.** Carry a pinch of salt when you go for an interview. See in Chapter 6 exactly what to do! Incredibly simple. but those who have tried it swear that this ancient formula works!

● **New Salt Magick For Bringing A Lover!** The person you want in your life can be yours. Also try this on someone you have parted with.

● **Diseases And Ailments Healed.** Salt Magick should not be used as a substitute for your doctor; but those who have tried it are convinced it helped them! Even total cures of serious health problems have been reported!

● **See Behind Walls; Read Other People's Minds; See The Future.** Chapter 3 reveals what to do!

You can bring love back into your life with this power! The one who doesn't want to know you now can have a change of heart once you use this potent magick! And *you don't need a photo or any article that belongs to this person for the magick to work!*

Also in this remarkable new book are the actual Salt Magick Rites that can help you: TRAVEL OUTSIDE YOUR BODY. An incredibly simple astral projection technique which the author swears by! . . . SUMMON YOUR PERSONAL GUARDIAN ANGEL TO MATERIALIZE BEFORE YOUR VERY EYES. It can happen! See Chapter 5 for creating the salt circle in which to see this phenomenon. *When he appears ask for what you want in life so that he may bring it to you!* . . . PROTECT YOUR HOME FROM FIRE AND THEFT. Simple New Salt Magick gives you not only protection but peace of mind . . . PSYCHIC DEFENCE. Has someone placed a curse on you? Are you a victim of evil black magick? *Salt magickally dissolves such evil vibrations and sets you free.* See Chapter 14.

Would you believe you can actually *control the weather through Salt Magick?* Author Jason Pike has kept records of using magick to control the elements and is convinced it works. This is the only Salt Magick Rite in the book which needs to be performed outdoors.

The uses of Salt Magick are practically without limit. All the ancient peoples — Egyptians, Hebrews, Greeks, Romans, to name a few — believe in its power; millions still do. Use the amazingly simple New Salt Magick Rites and find out for yourself!

Please send only £5.50 to:
Finbarr (OS), 16 Turketel Road,
Folkestone CT20 2PA.
Catalogue 50p. Callers at: 113 Dover Road, Folkestone.

TAURUS BORN PEOPLE

Birthdays between April 21st and May 21st inclusive. Your planet is Venus. Birthstone, emerald. Lucky day, Friday.

KEYNOTE FOR THE YEAR   Although you might not get yourself into gear as early in the year as you would wish, you do at least make significant progress before the end of the Spring. Finances tend to strengthen as the year progresses.

JANUARY   INFLUENCES: 1-2nd You might have to deal with the way that other people are behaving, using an unusual amount of tact. 14-15th Keeping a lid on your ambitions may be hard but is necessary. 30-31st Even confrontations could work to your advantage. OPPORTUNTIES: 16-17th A chance to improve your lot financially, even if it's hard to think how. LIMITING INFLUENCES: 21-22nd Others just do not seem able to appreciate your point of view as much as you would expect them to, so extra tact is very necessary.

FEBRUARY   INFLUENCES: 3-4th Confidence is high, especially when it comes to all professional matters. 12-13th Help comes in a practical sense, and possibly from a totally unexpected direction. 24-25th A little research would help before you commit yourself to projects that you know to be useful in the long-term. OPPORTUNITIES: 17-18th A new attitude would be useful when it comes to the more creative potential within you. LIMITING INFLUENCES: 11th A bad day for putting yourself in the position of taking risks that you know to be less than sensible.

MARCH   INFLUENCES: 2-3rd Attitudes are variable, though not quite as useful practically as they might be in a personal sense. 10-11th Combine your own efforts with those of friends for the best chance of success. 22-23rd Unusual coincidences come along, firing your enthusiasm for new personal ventures. OPPORTUNITIES: 26-27th A new inspiration in professional terms is something you are looking for, and can find at this time. LIMITING INFLUENCES: 6-7th Not everyone is equally helpful at this time, and you would do well to think before you speak out.

APRIL   INFLUENCES: 4-5th Not a period to be giving in to regrets of any sort, so stay optimistic. 12-13th A new incentive professionally allows you to make more of your life financially. 24-25th Rewards are coming in now, thanks to the very real effort you have been putting in recently. OPPORTUNITIES: 21-22nd Useful information now comes your way, especially if you have been looking for romance in your life. LIMITING INFLUENCES: 27th You are too variable in your approach to life and need to be careful what you say.

MAY   INFLUENCES: 1-2nd Tact and diplomacy are yours for the taking, but do you really want to be bothered? 10-11th All your energy is put in the direction of making things work better professionally. 27-28th A good time for using your creative potential, which is especially good now. OPPORTUNTIES: 16-17th Even apparently random events can now be turned to your advantage cash-wise. LIMITING INFLUENCES: 4-5th Reasoning powers are at an all-time low, so don't take any more chances than you really have to.

JUNE   INFLUENCES: 4-5th Confidence could be slightly higher, though there is no doubt that it is on the increase. 12-13th A new and more entertaining period now opens up, make the most of it. 24-25th When it comes to dealing with cash-flow problems, prevention is better than cure at present. OPPORTUNITIES: 16-17th Your mind is filled with tasks to be undertaken, though few of them intimidate you and help is at hand. LIMITING INFLUENCES: 29-30th You end the month with significantly less confidence than you entered it with.

JULY   INFLUENCES: 2-4th Create the right impression in social functions and new friendships. 19-20th You may decide that this would be a favourable interlude for taking some sort of a financial gamble, but exercise some care. 30-31st A revolutionary approach is necessary when dealing with people who fail to understand you. OPPORTUNITIES: 15-17th A snippet of news heard at this time can be turned very much to your advantage. LIMITING INFLUENCES: 22nd Beware of stretching your resources too much.

Please name FOULSHAM'S ALMANACK when replying to Advertisers

4 MILLION YEAR OLD MIRACLE OF NATURE
MARIE-SIMONE'S
GENUINE ROCK CRYSTAL PENDANT

Crystals, as well as being incredibly beautiful, have long been associated with amazing powers. Through the ages "crystal power" has been a respected force by many people. Crystals were created at the dawn of the earth. Millions of years on, geologists and scientists have developed ways to make these beautiful, jewel-like crystals available to you.

CONGRATULATIONS

We are giving you the opportunity to purchase a Genuine Rock Crystal Pendant set in a beautiful 24 carat Gold Plated Heart.
This Genuine Rock Crystal is designed to give:

☐ *GOOD LUCK*
☐ *GOOD SPIRITUAL HEALTH*
☐ *GOOD EMOTIONAL HEALTH*
☐ *WEALTH, HAPPINESS & WELL BEING*

This genuine Rock Crystal pendant, set in a beautiful 24 carat Gold-plated Heart and surrounded by flashing stones. It is truly a magnificent piece of jewellery you will be proud to wear, with its designer chain and delicate engraved backing. Such is the belief in the powers of these millions of years old Crystals that therapy clinics and centres are enjoying great success. "Crystal Power" has been a respected force by many people and used for healing and good luck for thousands of years. In the present day, geologists and scientists have developed ways to make these beautiful jewel-like Crystals available to you. The POWER of the Crystal makes all things possible – they are said to give off pure raw energy. Concentrate on what you want most in life and the Power of the Crystal will help you obtain it . . . may it be money, a new way to go ahead, finding a job, making new friends, or whatever is lacking in your life.
LET THE MYSTICAL POWER OF THE CRYSTAL BE THE ANSWER.

How the Magic of Miracle Power Crystals was discovered

The Miracle Power Crystal is an extremely rare type of rock crystal found only in scattered parts of the western United States. Geologists estimate that it is at least four million years old.
Several years ago, it became fashionable among the rich and famous to use these crystals in custom-made jewellery, along with diamonds, emeralds, rubies and other precious stones. As a result, the wealthy became owners of Miracle Power Crystals without even knowing it.
They soon noticed, however, that all kinds of wonderful things started happening to them! Some suspected that their new jewellery had something to do with their good fortune – but few guessed that the power really came from the Crystal, and the Crystal alone!
Finally, science perfected super-sensitive instruments that detect the dynamite energy waves given off by the crystals. They oscillate, vibrate and send out electromagnetic waves that surrounds the human body and attract *Good Luck . . . Money . . . New Friends . . . even Romance.*

AS QUOTED IN
THE SUN, Thursday, March 9th 1989

Forget diamonds. The way to a girl's heart in Hollywood these days is rock crystal. Stars are paying hundreds of thousands for the gleaming rock which, they say, has mystical powers. Shirley MacLaine claims it puts her in touch with the dead. She says: "Crystals have a divine purpose." And Ali McGraw says: "I'd rather have a crystal than a piece of sculpture. They are a very powerful reminder of God's universe."

Send £12 now to:
MARIE SIMONE
TOTTERIDGE VILLAGE
LONDON
N20 8PN

TO MARIE SIMONE, DEPT. OM95 C/M.
TOTTERIDGE VILLAGE, LONDON N20 8PN
Please send my Crystal Heart. I enclose £10 + £2 postage and handling.
(Make Cheque or Money Order Payable to Marie Simone).

Print Name...

Address ....

....

Post Code.................... Date of Birth ....

TAURUS BORN PEOPLE

AUGUST   INFLUENCES: 1-2nd A good start to the month, though some care is necessary when dealing with relatives. 10-11th Entertaining at home can be enjoyable and probably lucrative in some way too. 24-25th Standard responses to your work really will not do right now, so seek individuality. OPPORTUNITIES: 16-17th Make the most of an upward trend where family finances are concerned. LIMITING INFLUENCES: 5-6th Getting yourself into the right mood to deal with details is not at all easy, though relaxation is essential.

SEPTEMBER   INFLUENCES: 4-5th Confrontation can be avoided, though not without some effort in a family sense. 12-13th Be bold, even though this may not come all that easily. Friends help you. 22-25th A period for some deep reflection, though not a time of sadness or depression. OPPORTUNITES: 27-28th All your creative skills and personal charm are on display during this period. LIMITING INFLUENCES: 9-10th No matter what the effort you put in, you are likely to be held back by circumstances beyond your own control.

OCTOBER   INFLUENCES: 2-3rd Full of energy you now put yourself into every situation with great enthusiasm. 16-17th Results come from being in the right place at the right time. 28-29th Listen to what is being said, especially in a professional sense, some of it could turn out to be especially useful to you. OPPORTUNITIES: 13-14th Results are in the offing, mainly as a consequence of things you did in the past. LIMITING INFLUENCES: 22-23rd Doubting yourself and your own capabilities is almost inevitable now.

NOVEMBER   INFLUENCES: 1-2nd Standard and expected results are the best ones to still the doubts of others. 16-17th Probably feeling healthy and strong, you now take on new interests. 26-27th You may not feel very brave at this time, though others would see you as being so. OPPORTUNITIES: 13-14th Building greater security into your life is easy, making you feel much happier. LIMITING INFLUENCES: 20-21st Highs can turn into lows very easily now, so you need to try and keep your spirits up.

DECEMBER   INFLUENCES: 2-3rd Although tired at first, you still find the means to get plenty done, especially at home. 16-18th With more time to rest, you gain from the company of friends. 22-23rd New social contacts create a good atmosphere for the festivities. OPPORTUNITIES: 24-25th A Christmas period when you can spread yourself around a little and gain from the company of friends. LIMITING INFLUENCES: 19-20th Fatigue is something that you have to fight against now, if only because there is so much to do.

GEMINI BORN PEOPLE

Birthdays between May 22nd and June 21st inclusive. Your planet is Mercury. Birthstone, agate. Lucky day, Wednesday.

KEYNOTE FOR THE YEAR   Renewing your contact with aspects of the past turns out to be more important than you might imagine, though only in terms of what they can tell you about the future.

JANUARY   INFLUENCES: 1-2nd An excellent start to the year, full of happiness and social prospects. 13-14th Not everyone is equally helpful at this time, but you can find the ones who really are. 28-29th Your attitude is unusual, but is well understood by others. OPPORTUNITIES: 19-20th A good time for making gains in a romantic sense and with regard to some new friendships. LIMITING INFLUENCES: A standard response to the requirements of life are unlikely to work out for you now, flexibility is required.

Please name FOULSHAM'S ALMANACK when replying to Advertisers

I'm going to show you how we tap into psychic wisdom through sensitive response to our own intuitive powers

(The men can always eavesdrop)

Hi, I'm Cassandra Eason the psychic broadcaster, and these are my unique new books on self-development for women, based on the huge response to my regular phone-in programmes up and down the country. Thousands of case histories have confirmed that most psychic literature needs re-writing to take account of today's woman with her essentially modern problems - job/family conflict, boyfriends on the dole, elderly dependants etc. And these books highlight six kinds of Divination that focus the timeless force of intuition on these urgent practical issues.

For example, that old favourite **The Tarot.** Of course we all love those quaint medieval figures - but could their problems really be our problems? Yes... and their solutions too, if the symbolism is suitably updated. Same goes for **The Runes.** That much-respected Norse oracle wasn't exactly designed for single mums with mortgages. But those inner signals that show up among marked stones on a cloth still have plenty to tell us about the direction of our life's journey. Rune-magic can work in several media, the oldest being the **I-Ching** or Book of Changes dating from 3000 BC. Again, my book shows how the Yin and Yang combinations can spell out real answers to modern women's dilemmas. **Crystal Divination** is an effective harnessing of the mystic power of gemstones for restoring psychic harmony. (Plus, it's a lot of fun collecting these treasured crystals.) **Pendulum Dowsing** is a wonderfully sensitive pointer to your spiritual aims, while **Moon-readings** interpret many of those lunar influences on the body and mind, confirmed by science.

6 weeks to proficiency

My phone-ins also reveal that today's woman tends to be rushed off her feet, so these clear introductory courses can be mastered in just six weeks, equipping you for successful divination sessions on behalf of yourself and others.

Tarot Divination for Today's Woman £5.50
Rune Divination for Today's Woman £5.50
I-Ching Divination for Today's Woman £5.50
Crystal Divination for Today's Woman £5.50
Pendulum Dowsing for Today's Woman £5.50
Moon Divination for Today's Woman £5.50

Send Cheque/PO to Globe Book Services, Brunel Rd., Houndmills, Basingstoke, Hants, RG21 2XS. Prices include p&p. Allow 28 days for delivery.

GEMINI BORN PEOPLE

FEBRUARY INFLUENCES: 3-4th You decide to carry almost any issue through to its logical conclusion during this period. 16-17th Although less dogmatic than of late, you still know what you want and how to go about getting it. 26-27th Create a good social atmosphere and do only those things that you know will please others too if you want the best results. OPPORTUNITIES: 13-14th Confidence is high and allows you to be even more effective in your efforts. LIMITING INFLUENCES: 25th Almost any grass looks greener now, but it isn't in reality.

MARCH INFLUENCES: 2-3rd Love and romance are paramount in your mind, almost to the point of obsession. 12-13th Some confusion at this time, but even these can be turned to your advantage in the end. 29-30th Responsibilities press in on you, and the best thing that you can do is to share them around a little. OPPORTUNITIES: 17-18th A gradual climb to a better financial position begins during this period. LIMITING INFLUENCES: 26th General confidence takes a nose-dive, though possibly not for long.

APRIL INFLUENCES: 4-5th Attitudes are variable, but mainly those coming from others, whilst you remain certain. 16-17th Potential exists for changing professional aspects of your life that you do not care for. 29-30th End the month on a high note by remaining as sociable as life will allow you to be. OPPORTUNITIES: 14-15th Better financial prospects see you able to spoil yourself a little. LIMITING INFLUENCES: 27th It is too easy to take exception to what others are saying quite casually and without any real malice.

MAY INFLUENCES: 1-2nd You show a remarkable ability to stand out in any crowd and to make a good impression. 12-13th Relatives and friends are in a good position to do you some important favours. 27-28th An unusual attitude is evident, though it may turn out to be distinctly useful at some stage. OPPORTUNITIES: Make up your mind about career changes whilst fortune favours your decisions. LIMITING INFLUENCES: 22-23rd It is likely that you are feeling more lonely than usual, perhaps even isolated.

JUNE INFLUENCES: 2-3rd The past catches up with you at this time, though certainly not in any negative sort of way. 19-20th Confronting past issues is something you now excel at and little brings fear to you. 27-28th You are now able to come through difficulties that seemed insurmountable. OPPORTUNITIES: 22-23rd Gains come from the direction of both relatives and friends. LIMITING INFLUENCES: 29th The attitude of some people is confusing to say the least and may not improve immediately.

JULY INFLUENCES: 1-2nd Don't turn down the possibility of travel, even at the last minute. 12-14th Assertive and very outspoken in your opinions, some tact is more than necessary. 21-22nd Projects close to your heart should be pursued at all costs now that circumstances are on your side. OPPORTUNITIES: 10-11th A fortunate time for seeking professional advice and for taking it on board. LIMITING INFLUENCES: 25th Some restrictions are inevitable, even when you work against them.

AUGUST INFLUENCES: 2-3rd It might be quicker to do things for yourself rather than getting others too involved. 12-13th You are thinking about things very deeply at present, maybe just a little too much so. 24-25th Attitudes are variable but you can do much to help yourself in a professional sense. OPPORTUNITIES: 19-20th Back your hunches over financial transactions and don't be put off. LIMITING INFLUENCES: 27-28th Leave behind you concepts that are no longer of any use.

SEPTEMBER INFLUENCES: 1-2nd A bright and breezy time, good for getting yourself out and about. 12-13th If you have been standing on some of the qualities of your own nature, now is the time to let them show. 23-24th Confidence is on the increase, and there is plenty to get done in a practical sense on these days. OPPORTUNITIES: 17-18th Difficult jobs are easy to undertake now. LIMITING INFLUENCES: 27-28th The bottom may be inclined to drop out of some of your most important plans.

OCTOBER INFLUENCES: 2-4th Concentrating on the job in hand may not be at all easy, though it is necessary. 16-17th Bring others round to your point of view with a mixture of enthusiasm and tact if you can. 24-25th A remarkable time if you pick up on all the possibilities that stand around you in a general sense. OPPORTUNITIES: 19-20th Improve your financial lot by being sensible in the sort of financial transactions you undertake. LIMITING INFLUENCES: 27-28th People fail to follow your reasoning and you must be patient with them.

YOU COULD SOLVE ALL YOUR PROBLEMS IN 24 HOURS FLAT!

Money, Love, Health, Happiness — What's your toughest problem? I personally GUARANTEE that my amazing discovery can work like a charm for you . . . *OR I'LL GIVE YOU YOUR MONEY BACK!*

I want to be honest with you right from the very start.

I really can't explain how my **Problem-Solver** discovery miraculously destroyed my heartaches so quickly.

But I can tell you this: *It REALLY works!*

Just a few years ago, nothing was going right. I was BADLY troubled by one problem after another.

My husband and I needed a pot of money desperately. I was going into the hospital for an operation. My three children were having a tough time at school. I was out of my mind with worry and depressed all the time.

Worse yet, my 80-year-old mother took sick a thousand miles away and I didn't even have enough for the 'plane fare.

As you can imagine, I was a physical and mental wreck. I walked around every single day waiting and praying for something good to happen to me. Something, **anything,** that would lift me and my family out of this "ball and chain" rut. It was the lowest, deepest point of my life — with NO hope of changing it!

THEN A MIRACLE HAPPENED THE PROBLEM-SOLVER

Just as I was about to walk off the deep end, it happened. Suddenly, with absolutely no warning at all, I stumbled upon the **Problem-Solver**. I'll remember that day as long as I live. Everything started to turn around FAST!

How I discovered it is a secret I promised never to reveal. Not even to my husband or my closest girl-friend. So please don't even try to get it out of me. I won't tell you.

What I can reveal to you now is this: How the **Problem-Solver** started eliminating all my problems, day-by-day, until every single one of them was gone from my life FOREVER!

** *INCREDIBLE!* My husband started to make THOUSANDS AND THOUSANDS OF POUNDS and for the first time since we were married, we were actually banking money . . . and lots of it!

** *INCREDIBLE!* My hospital stay was successful and now I feel better than ever and I'm even playing tennis!

** *INCREDIBLE!* I got out of my depression. My mother is no longer a problem and to celebrate we went for the best second honeymoon ever!

** *INCREDIBLE!* My luck changed! Everything I touched turned to GOLD. Even my kids see the BIG difference in me.

I'm richer, healthier, luckier and happier than I've ever been in twenty years. Everything looks great now. I owe everything to my **Problem-Solver.**

ITS FANTASTIC!

Unbelievably, my **Problem-Solver** never quits doing its remarkable job for me. It just keeps on working day-after-lovely day . . . NONSTOP!

For instance: (1) My son and his wife gave me a darling little grandson. (2) I've finally found a way to slim down painlessly. (3) My two girls finished school and have excellent-paying jobs. (4) The Mercedes I've always wanted was recently delivered right to my front door . . . paid in full!

To tell you the truth, I can't believe it myself. Every day something else "GREAT" happens to me. Is my **Problem-Solver** working? You bet your life!

IT WILL SOLVE ALL YOUR PROBLEMS, TOO!

Would you like to get rid of all your problems just like I did? Would you like to have everything coming your way? Answer "Yes," and I'll send you a replica of my sensational **Problem-Solver.**

I want to send it to you RIGHT NOW — so you can have it with you EVERY SINGLE DAY OF YOUR LIFE — FOREVER!

That's right! I want you to keep it permanently to help solve ALL problems in life — no matter what they are or how many you have.

Just sit back and imagine the thrill when the **Problem-Solver** starts to work for you. It's amazing powers will make you the envy of all your friends and relatives.

I'll be glad to send you the **Problem-Solver** in a privately marked package for just £12 on my unconditional lifetime money-back guarantee!

As soon as the **Problem-Solver** arrives, try it out on your most pressing problem. Prove to yourself that what I've said is 100% true, or just send it back to me for a full GUARANTEED REFUND anytime.

Don't live another day without the **Problem-Solver.** Order RIGHT NOW for prompt delivery.

GUARANTEED FOR LIFE!

When you receive the **Problem-Solver**, expect to experience MONEY, LOVE, HEALTH, OR HAPPINESS — beyond your wildest dreams!

With your **Problem-Solver** I will send you also my latest exclusive Work: "Successful Living", over 2,000 words, just for you, based on your date of Birth . . . may be you be Gemini, Libra or any other Sign of the Zodiac.

This work is for YOU . . . how to obtain Luck, Happiness, Fortune.

This work and your **Problem-Solver**, together, is the Luckiest package you could wish for. Do not hesitate, order NOW, TODAY! You may bless the day you did!

MAIL AT ONCE

MARIE-SIMONE, Dept OM95P
TOTTERIDGE VILLAGE
LONDON N20 8PN

RUSH THE PROBLEM-SOLVER

YES! I enclose just £12. Rush my **Problem-Solver** right away. It MUST work for me or you will return my money ANYTIME without quibble or question.

Print name ....

Address ....

....

....

Birthdate ....

GEMINI BORN PEOPLE

NOVEMBER: INFLUENCES: 4-5th Retrace your steps a little in order to realise that progress sometimes comes from looking back. 19-20th Friends are a little out of order with some of the things they are saying, though some of their reasoning makes sense. 29-30th Routines take on an interesting new feel. OPPORTUNITIES: 25-27th It is towards projects associated with work that you can turn your mind now, and successes follow. LIMITING INFLUENCES: 23-24th Not everyone automatically agrees with what you have to say at this time.

DECEMBER INFLUENCES: 3-4th Attitude is all-important, especially when you are dealing with people who are naturally obstinate. 12-13th Someone is not too pleased with you, though you can turn the tables simply by speaking sensibly. 26-27th New people and places play an important role in your ultimate decision making. OPPORTUNITIES: 22-23rd It is the practical aspects of life that captivate you at present and which can be utilised. LIMITING INFLUENCES: 19-20th A little stupidity is something you can forgive yourself, but not masses of it.

CANCER BORN PEOPLE

Birthdays between June 22nd and July 22nd inclusive. Your planet is the Moon. Birthstone, ruby. Lucky day, Monday.

KEYNOTE FOR THE YEAR   A realistic approach to the beginning of the year makes you more content to allow life to take its own course. Compromise is important when it comes to dealing with relatives and friends.

JANUARY INFLUENCES: 1-2nd People seem determined to try your patience, though you take no real notice. 7-9th If you are worrying about social arrangements, try to stop. 31st A positive end to the month, with much optimism. OPPORTUNITIES: 22-23rd People who have irritated you in the past now come round to thinking the way you do. LIMITING INFLUENCES: 6-7th Relatives and friends alike can be irritating and awkward to sort out.

FEBRUARY INFLUENCES: 1-2nd Friends can be critical but you still have to choose for yourself. 5-7th The charitable side of your nature allows you to do some good for others. 17-18th Confidence levels appear to be low and yet you get much done now. OPPORTUNITIES: 22-23rd As well as meeting people from the past, new contacts can be very essential. LIMITING INFLUENCES: 9-10th One or two small worries associated with home and family are easy to blow up out of all proportion.

MARCH INFLUENCES: 1-2nd One or two practical difficulties at the start of March can be avoided if you think first. 7-8th You need to get your personal message across and can do so extremely effectively at any time now. 20-21st A quieter Cancerian greets the world for a day or two as you become more thoughtful. OPPORTUNITIES: 26-27th Tedious jobs are out of the way and now you can really concentrate on your own life. LIMITING INFLUENCES: 13-14th You might be a little insensitive to the needs of others and so will have to tread especially carefully.

APRIL INFLUENCES: 3-4th You are in a peace-loving mood and unlikely to encourage arguments. 10-11th People might misunderstand your motives, so tread carefully. 17-18th An urge for personal freedom makes routines tedious. 24-26th Practical necessities come easier now. 30th Give and take in relationships is very important. OPPORTUNITIES: 28-29th Freedom from the restrictions of the past makes this time quite special, for yourself and others. LIMITING INFLUENCES: 15-16th You show a tendency to be impatient that can cause one or two problems practically.

MAY INFLUENCES: 2-3rd Don't expect too much of yourself until later in the month. 10-11th A period when recreation and your social life will be to the forefront of your mind. 23-24th A very romantic interlude lifts this interlude in May. 31st Tell others how you really feel about things. OPPORTUNITIES: 5-6th Most new possibilities are worth a second look now. LIMITING INFLUENCES: 19-20th Achieving a genuinely fair standpoint is not easy at this time.

Please name FOULSHAM'S ALMANACK when replying to Advertisers

THE EYE OF HORUS

(you will see silver – you will see gold)

This could be the world's oldest and most powerful lucky charm

From the beginning of time, the eye has been a symbol of good luck. The eye on the ships of the ancient Greeks, (still in use today). The third eye from the monastery's of Tibet and the **"Eye of Horus'**, used by the Pharaoh's in Egypt 4,000 years ago. All were credited with the **power** to bring good luck and fortune to the owner of this remarkable Talisman. Today, we call this power positive thought. The ability to change our lives and bring **wealth** and **happiness** within our grasp.

NOW <u>YOU</u> HAVE THE CHANCE TO POSSESS THIS HANDCRAFTED TALISMAN.

YOU WILL SEE SILVER — Silver is the metal of protection against evil and denotes purity.

YOU WILL SEE GOLD — Used in the highest and most important magical ceremonies. It symbolizes **riches,** wisdom, life and perfection. It is said to protect against disease.

Each Talisman will be signed on the reverse by "Merman" your guarantee of a Talisman that has been carefully made in the correct manner. The **"EYE OF HORUS"** is a Talisman hand crafted especially for you. (Each one will be slightly different.)

Real Silver and **Real Gold** is used and you will agree that super value will be yours.

You will receive a leaflet explaining how you can use the **"Eye of Horus"** to your best advantage.

This remarkable Talisman, craftsman made from solid Silver and Gold (not plated) is available to you for just £12.00 incl. postage. You will also receive a **FREE** 18″ chain or **FREE** plated keyring. Please choose which you prefer. — The **"EYE OF THE HORUS"** is obtainable only from "MERMAN", who else cares as much. If you wish you may write to me, telling me of your wishes, or just use the order form below.

YES, I WANT THE **'EYE OF HORUS'** TO BRING ME GOOD FORTUNE. I ENCLOSE MY CHEQUE/P.O. FOR £12.00 MADE PAYABLE TO "MERMAN".

PLEASE TICK YOUR CHOICE

18″ CHAIN ☐ KEY RING ☐

PLEASE PRINT

NAME ....

ADDRESS ....

....

.... POSTCODE ....

POST TO: **Merman (E.H.), 1 Doneley Court, Berrycombe Road, Bodmin, Cornwall PL31 2NX**

CANCER BORN PEOPLE

JUNE INFLUENCES: 2-3rd You are really in the mood to have a good natter and air your opinions. 9th Surprising invitations or opportunities, together with some unusual people crop up. 17-18th Renewed confidence is possible regarding people that have let you down in the past. 24-25th All topics are grist to the mill when it comes to a family discussion. OPPORTUNITIES: 10-11th Recent efforts begin to show fortunate trends and gains generally. LIMITING INFLUENCES: 21-22nd If you extend yourself too much mentally and physically difficulties could follow.

JULY INFLUENCES: 2-3rd A slightly deep and secretive Cancerian is likely to greet the start of July. 9-10th Get all tedious jobs out of the way as soon as you can at this time. 18-19th Your effort, combined with that of your friends, can work wonders in your immediate environment. 29th A day to rest and to make plans for journeys that take place at this stage. OPPORTUNITIES: 11-12th Look for comfort and make your home surroundings more luxurious. LIMITING INFLUENCES: 25-27th Friends can be quite difficult to deal with and seem determined to cause you problems.

AUGUST INFLUENCES: 2-3rd A practical couple of days is what you will be seeking and managing to find. 12th Attitudes towards others are variable at this time. 14-15th The more unconventional you manage to be, the better things turn to your advantage. 19th Try your hand at work at home or perhaps creative pursuits of some other sort. OPPORTUNTIES: 16-17th Variations in the way that you do things makes for an interesting interlude to the month. LIMITING INFLUENCES: 29-30th Too much concern for other people can be as much of a problem as any you encounter now.

SEPTEMBER INFLUENCES: 1-2nd Important decisons may have to wait but fun is for the taking. 6-7th Talk about what is important to you at the present time. 13-15th Invitations come in thick and fast. 24-25th Combined projects are better at the moment than solo efforts of any sort, so look for as much cooperation as you are able to find. OPPORTUNITIES: 17-18th Re-plays of past events turn out much more in your favour this time around. LIMITING INFLUENCES: 4-5th Any deviation from the absolute truth could lead you into problems.

OCTOBER INFLUENCES: 2-3rd A period of significant optimism begins at this time. 11-12th Health issues are on your mind, though there is little to worry about. 16-.17th Good luck is a matter of taking your life in your own hands at the present time. 22-23rd Down in the mouth friends are wanting to turn to you for all sorts of support. OPPORTUNITIES: 20-21st It is important to allow fresh starts to have your full attention now and to make the most of them. LIMITING INFLUENCES: 8-9th Don't speculate too much right now or losses could turn out to be the result.

NOVEMBER INFLUENCES: 1-2nd Creativity, combined with good powers of observation, stand you in good stead. 6-7th The depth of your present nature is hard for others to comprehend. 17-18th By helping others out as much as you can you discover more about yourself. 24th Not everyone agrees with your point of view but they are willing to listen all the same. OPPORTUNITIES: 22-23rd Slow and really steady persistence all pay great dividends soon. LIMITING INFLUENCES: 8-9th A lack of emotional strength can leave you quite vulnerable to slight depression.

DECEMBER INFLUENCES: 1-2nd A dynamic start to the month, though less than practical in some ways. 9-10th You are home-loving and warm in your attitudes to those who need you. 20-21st Rules and regulations really begin to get on your nerves prior to Christmas. 29-30th Big ideas lead to quite remarkable adventures. OPPORTUNITIES: 26-27th You bring great flair to bear in all your desires. LIMITING INFLUENCES: 12-13th Confidence to do the things that you normally would not think about at all now seems to be lacking and you need a little more belief in yourself.

Please name FOULSHAM'S ALMANACK when replying to Advertisers

DEVASTATING
LOVE SPELLS!

Not a sex manual but *33 powerful* occult spells. Results sometimes seen *within hours*, says author Paul Summers! He says these spells can make a person *like putty in your hands!* *No* calling up spirits, *no* hard-to-get materials: these spells are simple, safe, and above all, says the author, *fast working!* Contents: **Make A Disinterested Party Suddenly Want You!** . . . **Make A Disenchanted Lover Contact You!** . . . **Make Yourself Irresistible To Others!** . . . **Bring Back A Spouse!** These spells *never before in print!* Amazing results reported by readers! Only £6.95.

EXPRESS TELEPATHY

Never before in print psychic spells for getting people to do what you want — without them knowing! In this report P. Summers says: **You can get immediate attention and respect when you enter a room** . . . **Get someone to 'phone you — immediately!** . . . **Make a complete stranger attracted to you!** . . . **Give psychic healing to a person miles away!** No months of study required; start *within minutes!* Only £5.

NEW AGE MONEY SPELLS

You can **magically turn your purse or wallet into a magic magnet** for attracting cash, says occultist Paul Summers! He reveals *never before in print* spells for magically 'charging' your cheque book; also magic spells for the racing track, stock market, bingo, etc. Seems crazy, but readers report amazing results! These spells *very simple* — and safe! Only £5.

HOW TO FIND YOUR TRUE SOUL MATE

Is it really possible to find a person with whom you can have *real* harmony? Everyone has a true soul mate, says J. Cullinan, author of this report, and he shows how to attract this person into your life. Only £3.

SECRETS OF 'FINGER MAGIC'

Revealed by I. Currey, an occult Adeptus Minor, 'Finger Magic' requires no long rituals or equipment, and can even be used by one in a crowded room or bus! It can achieve for you: **An increase in pay!** . . . **Fulfilment of sexual desires!** . . . **Wins in lotteries, bingo, and horses!** . . . **Settlement of debts!** . . . **Healing of a sick friend!** . . . **Meet the perfect mate!** . . . **Heal a sick animal!** . . . **Turn an enemy into a friend!** . . . **Lose weight!** . . . **Win a court action!** . . . **End insomnia!** . . . **Bring harmony into the home!** . . . **Stop a family feud!** . . . **Make a neighbour move away!** . . . **Control children!** Only £4.

NOTE THESE REPORTS ARE NOT BOOKS BUT SHORT, TO THE POINT, 'HOW TO' GUIDES. THEY ARE NOT AVAILABLE IN ANY SHOP, BUT ONLY BY MAIL DIRECT FROM PUBLISHERS. Send cheque P.O. to:

FINBARR SPECIAL REPORTS (O)

16 Turketel Road, Folkestone, Kent CT20 2PA

We use discreet packaging. Orders usually sent within 48 hours. If need is urgent write 'PRIORITY' on the face of envelope and add 40p. Catalogue 50p. Callers at 113 Dover Road, Folkestone. *We have advertised in Old Moore's since 1975 — order with confidence!*

The Holy Squares of Divine Magic

'HOLY SQUARES SAVED MY LIFE!'
Author Jason Pike had a serious health problem: 'The Holy Squares led me to important information which I believe saved my life'.

'LARGE BLOOD CLOT DISAPPEARED!'
Mr Pike's friend was seriously ill; but a Holy Square made the seemingly impossible happen!

'MY GUARDIAN ANGEL APPEARED BEFORE ME!'
— so reported Mr Pike after he held a Holy Square in his hand. 'It was an extraordinary experience'.

MAGIC FORMULA FOR CHRISTIANS, MUSLIMS, JEWS!
(You can even be atheist.) But it is important you speak the words that control the Squares correctly — this is what counts!

After 700 years the fabled Holy Squares of Abramelin the Jew have been simplified for the modern person! Abramelin was a great 14th century magician who, it was alleged, received visions of the Holy Squares from God Himself! These squares were believed to have held *awesome* power — but, alas, few could access their power! Even though the Squares were published *virtually no one could perform the instructions because of their extraordinary complexity!*

But — at last — thanks to divine revelation to advanced occultist Jason Pike, the instructions for using the Holy Squares have now been **made simple and practical**! But their power remains *intact* because Mr Pike and his students have received staggering results as a consequence of using them!

Absolutely no experience is required to awaken the divine magic of the Holy Squares! But Mr Pike urges you not to use them if you *are not serious in your intent!* For within these Squares lay *seven centuries of fabled magic power* — which is not to be taken lightly!

132 Holy Squares are supplied, including:
Holy Squares for receiving endless love and devotion from your spouse
Holy Square for receiving love and devotion of family
Holy Square for receiving the love of a specific person
Holy Square for receiving the love of a widow
Holy Square for receiving the love of an older man
Holy Square for making two people quarrel and split up
Holy Square for causing bad feeling between specific females
Holy Square for making you look older than your age
Holy Square for making you look younger than your age
Holy Square for finding stolen property
Holy Square for becoming an exceptionally good swimmer
Holy Square for finding out people's secrets
Holy Square for mastering a foreign language
Four Holy Squares for conversing with those who have died
Holy Square for becoming invisible
Nineteen Holy Squares for receiving large amounts of money
Holy Square to cure agrophobia
Holy Square to cure sore palms and feet
Holy Square to cure battle wounds
Holy Square to cure excessive fluid in body
Holy Square to cure migraine, fear of heights, sea sickness
Holy Square to cure claustrophobia, influenza, cramp
Holy Square for detecting true or false friends
Holy Square for learning about the past of an enemy
Holy Square for foreseeing fierce storms; where and when they will occur
Holy Square for protecting your home
Holy Square for safe mountain climbing
Holy Square to control weather conditions; to make it rain
Holy Square to render a curse ineffective

To receive (all) Holy Squares (in one book) send £5 to:
Finbarr (OQ), 16 Turketel Road, Folkestone CT20 2PA.
Callers: 113 Dover Road, Folkestone.

LEO BORN PEOPLE

Birthdays between July 23rd and August 23rd inclusive. Your planet is the Sun. Birthstone, sapphire. Lucky day, Sunday.

KEYNOTE FOR THE YEAR   Set out your stall just as dynamic as your positive sign allows and don't allow yourself to be thwarted in your objectives, no matter how adventurous they may turn out to be.

JANUARY   INFLUENCES: 1-2nd You are quite settled at the start of the year and well able to sort out priorities. 16-17th It might not be all that easy to sort out how you feel about others. 30-31st End the month with the same sort of optimism that was present at its start. OPPORTUNITIES: 7-8th The chance comes to spend time with your family and to get the most from friends too. LIMITING INFLUENCES: 22-23rd Frustrations are short in duration but do need looking at sensibly.

FEBRUARY   INFLUENCES: 2-3rd Be adventurous and don't allow your plans to be thwarted by negative types. 16-17th New financial prospects are in store, but watch cash just for the moment. 27-28th This would not be a good time for starting any arguments. OPPORTUNITIES: 5-6th If there are any favours that you are needing, this has to be the best time to ask for them. LIMITING INFLUENCES: 18-19th Make certain that you have your facts right before you start to put pressure on others.

MARCH   INFLUENCES: 1-2nd Keep your eyes open because there are some less than reliable types to be dealt with. 16-17th Not a good time to take any chances with life. 29-30th You now have the ability to make up your mind almost instantly and to deal with the consequences. OPPORTUNITIES: 5-6th Dealing with certain aspects of your life that have been problematic is your job at this time. LIMITING INFLUENCES: 19-20th You need more self-discipline.

APRIL   INFLUENCES: 1-2nd Your social life is likely to be running more or less as you would wish it to. 18-19th Most of your decisions are based on life experience, though intuition is also important now. 22nd An atmospheric time, with plenty to do practically too. 29-30th An end to the month that could bring some surprising news. OPPORTUNITIES: 27-28th Looking after your personal security now becomes a must. LIMITING INFLUENCES: 14-15th A lack of excitement makes you look around.

MAY   INFLUENCES: 2-3rd The most casual of chance meetings turns out to be to your advantage. 14-15th Although you may not want to cheat others, you may have to explain yourself in order to avoid doing so. 27-28th Arguments that cannot be won are a waste of time, so stay away from them. OPPORTUNITIES: 25-26th You might find that there is a little more money about than you expected. LIMITING INFLUENCES: 12-14th Not everyone you come across is to be trusted, so try to exercise a little care with strangers.

JUNE   INFLUENCES: 2-3rd Personal relationships take some careful handling, but you are in the mood to be sensible. 12-14th Life looks interesting and there is plenty to demand your time. 25-26th Even the arrival of apparent difficulties does little to change your optimistic view-point. OPPORTUNITIES: 21-22nd Getting your own way is not hard, though it does take some effort. LIMITING INFLUENCES: 9-10th For a couple of days you do not appear to be looking at things with quite your usual sense.

JULY   INFLUENCES: 1-2nd Personal relationships may need looking at very carefully for a day or two. 11-12th The most unusual circumstances come your way and most of them work to your distinct advantage. 28-29th You look towards social prospects with a great deal of enthusiasm. OPPORTUNITIES: 19-20th You now have plenty of confidence to take on new enterprises and make them work for you. LIMITING INFLUENCES: 30-31st Accepting second-best from yourself is something that you might have to get used to for a while.

AUGUST   INFLUENCES: 2-3rd This would be an ideal time for thinking about travel, or perhaps changes around your home. 15-16th Although a quiet period, there is no reason to believe that things work against your best interests. 29-30th Greater incentive to follow your own intuition is now evident. OPPORTUNITIES: 21-22nd Make the most of new people and places who come into your life right now. LIMITING INFLUENCES: 25-26th Much of your time is spent looking after the needs of others.

   Cont'd on p. 48

Please name FOULSHAM'S ALMANACK when replying to Advertisers

prediction

BRITAIN'S BIGGEST-
SELLING MONTHLY
MAGAZINE IN
ITS FIELD

All about
YOU

ESTABLISHED
FOR NEARLY
60 YEARS

◆ ASTROLOGY – TAROT – PALMISTRY
GRAPHOLOGY – DREAM INTERPRETATIONS ◆

These are just some of the methods used to interpret character and events in life. Prediction magazine covers a whole host of other subjects ranging from premonitions and divination to mind-over-matter. Every issue of Prediction magazine carries a sixteen-page astrology section including Sun sign forecasts for the month ahead plus book reviews, a directory of pyschics, consultants, societies and much, much more.

DON'T MISS AN ISSUE!

Available from all leading newsagents and on post free subscription in the U.K. Published on the second Friday of every month. For a sample copy of the latest issue send a cheque or postal order for £1.50 and your name and address to: Prediction Magazine, Link House, Dingwall Avenue, Croydon CR9 2TA. Telephone 081-686 2599. *LH* A Link House Magazine

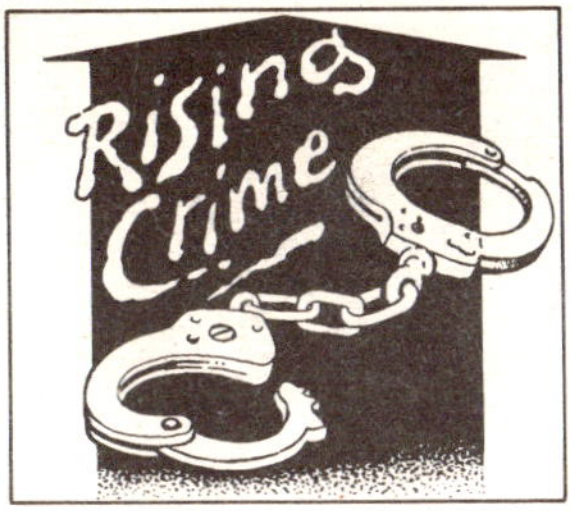

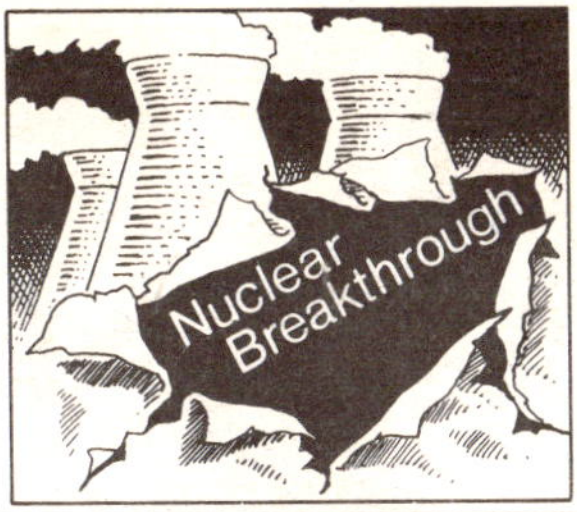

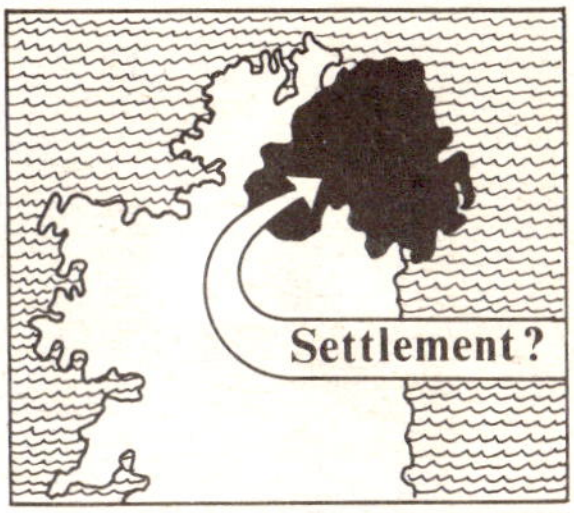

JANUARY

For High Water add, for Bristol 5h. 30m., Hull 4h. 23m., Leith 0h. 43m., and for Dublin sub. 2h. 21m., Greenock 1h. 22m., Liverpool 2h. 29m.

D of M	D of W	Sundays, Festivals Special Events, etc., for 1995	Sun Rises R Sets S	High Water at London Bridge		Moon at London		Weather
				Morn.	After.	Rises	Sets	
			h. m.	h. m.	h. m.	h. m.	h. m.	
1	☉	1st Sun. after Christmas	R 8 06	1 08	13 34	7 38	16 36	The New Year sees the coldest spell of Winter with severe frosts and snow. It turns milder during the second half, but there will be the occasional blustery shower.
2	M	Bank Holiday	S16 02	1 57	14 23	8 22	17 53	
3	Tu	Josiah Wedgwood d. 1795	R 8 05	2 44	15 11	8 58	19 10	
4	W	Louis Braille b. 1809	S16 05	3 29	15 56	9 28	20 25	
5	Th	Battle of Nancy 1477	R 8 05	4 11	16 39	9 54	21 38	
6	F	Epiphany/Twelfth Night	S16 07	4 53	17 23	10 17	22 48	
7	S	Emperor Hirohito d. 1989	R 8 04	5 34	18 05	10 39	23 55	
8	☉	1st Sunday after Epiphany	S16 10	6 15	18 50	11 02	—	
9	M	Plough Monday	R 8 03	7 01	19 41	11 26	1 01	
10	Tu	Rod Stewart b. 1945	S16 12	7 59	20 41	11 53	2 05	
11	W	United Belgium 1790	R 8 02	9 05	21 49	12 24	3 07	
12	Th	Tex Ritter b. 1907	S16 15	10 21	23 02	13 01	4 06	
13	F	Dallas Airport op. 1974	R 8 01	11 34	23 59	13 43	5 01	
14	S	Richard Briers b. 1934	S16 18	—	12 25	14 33	5 50	
15	☉	2nd Sunday after Epiphany	R 7 59	0 43	13 05	15 29	6 34	
16	M	Cliff Thorburn b. 1948	S16 21	1 22	13 43	16 31	7 12	
17	Tu	Emp. Theodosius I. d. 395	R 7 58	2 00	14 21	17 37	7 45	
18	W	German Empire procl. 1871	S16 24	2 37	14 59	18 46	8 14	
19	Th	Earl of Surrey exec. 1547	R 7 56	3 13	15 36	19 57	8 40	
20	F	Barbara Stanwyck d. 1990	S16 28	3 49	16 12	21 08	9 04	
21	S	Martin Shaw b. 1945	R 7 54	4 22	16 49	22 21	9 28	
22	☉	3rd Sunday after Epiphany	S16 31	4 57	17 27	23 36	9 52	
23	M	Royal Exchange op. 1571	R 7 51	5 34	18 09	—	10 19	
24	Tu	Rand. Churchill d. 1895	S16 34	6 18	19 00	0 51	10 50	
25	W	Burns Night	R 7 49	7 15	20 07	2 06	11 28	
26	Th	Australia Day/St Paula	S16 38	8 35	21 27	3 19	12 13	
27	F	Giuseppe Verdi d. 1901	R 7 42	10 00	22 45	4 26	13 09	
28	S	Diet of Worms began 1521	S16 42	11 21	23 56	5 24	14 14	
29	☉	4th Sunday after Epiphany	R 7 44	—	12 29	6 13	15 26	
30	M	St Basil	S16 45	0 56	13 25	6 53	16 42	
31	Tu	Old Chinese New Year	R 7 41	1 46	14 14	7 26	17 59	

MOON'S PHASES JANUARY 1995

		Days	*Hrs.*	*Mins.*
●	New Moon	1	10	56
☽	First Quarter	8	15	46
○	Full Moon	16	20	26
☾	Last Quarter	24	4	58
●	New Moon	30	22	48

All times on this page are GMT

PREDICTIONS

The year opens with a New Moon on the 1st in Capricorn. Mars will be in a square with Pluto, Jupiter and Saturn. This represents a combative start to the year. The public mood will be dominated by concern over declining morality, rising crime levels and the threat of terrorism. The chances for peace moves remain high, and there will be further steps for reconciliation between Israel and the Arab states. In the UK the Labour Party could be moving towards further constitutional changes reflecting recent alterations in the leadership of the Party and also the needs of the next election.

The Full Moon on the 16th falls in Cancer, in opposition to Uranus, encouraging radical political movements and bringing a high chance of a further breakthrough in nuclear technology. This is also the first of several months which highlights the prospect of airline deregulation and cheaper flights. In the UK there will now be major steps towards what will hopefully be a final constitutional settlement in Northern Ireland, but if matters are not settled by the end of March the prospects of success will diminish. From the USA there could also be news of a major technological breakthrough, probably in nuclear fusion.

The Great Yorkshire Chase at Doncaster may be won by the favourite.

The tidal predictions for London Bridge have been computed by the Proudman Oceanographic Laboratory.

Copyright reserved.

Predicted Russian Disintegration 1990

FEBRUARY

For High Water add, for Bristol 5h. 30m., Hull 4h. 23m., Leith 0h. 43m., and for Dublin sub. 2h. 21m., Greenock 1h. 22m., Liverpool 2h. 29m.

D of M	D of W	Sundays, Festivals Special Events, etc., for 1995	Sun Rises R Sets S	High Water at London Bridge Morn.	High Water at London Bridge After.	Moon at London Rises	Moon at London Sets	Weather
			h. m.	h. m.	h. m.	h. m.	h. m.	
1	W	1st day of Ramadân	S16 49	2 31	14 58	7 54	19 13	
2	Th	Sid Vicious d. 1979	R 7 38	3 12	15 39	8 19	20 26	
3	F	St Blaze	S16 52	3 51	16 18	8 42	21 36	
4	S	Yalta Conference b'n 1945	R 7 34	4 29	16 55	9 06	22 44	
5	☙	5th Sunday after Epiphany	S16 56	5 04	17 31	9 30	23 50	
6	M	Eliz. II accession 1952	R 7 31	5 41	18 09	9 56	—	
7	Tu	Portland Vase broken 1845	S17 00	6 20	18 53	10 25	0 53	
8	W	Dame Edith Evans b. 1888	R 7 28	7 11	19 45	10 59	1 53	
9	Th	St Apollonia	S17 03	8 13	20 48	11 39	2 50	
10	F	New Dehli offic. op. 1931	R 7 24	9 23	21 57	12 26	3 42	
11	S	Lourdes miracle 1858	S17 07	10 43	23 16	13 19	4 28	
12	☙	Septuagesima Sunday	R 7 21	11 52	—	14 18	5 09	
13	M	Mata Hari arrested 1917	S17 11	0 13	12 39	15 23	5 44	
14	Tu	St Valentine's Day	R 7 17	0 57	13 19	16 31	6 15	
15	W	Britain went decimal 1971	S17 14	1 38	13 59	17 42	6 43	
16	Th	John McEnroe b. 1957	R 7 13	2 16	14 37	18 55	7 08	
17	F	Geronimo d. 1909	S17 18	2 52	15 15	20 09	7 33	
18	S	Alessandro Volta b. 1745	R 7 09	3 27	15 51	21 24	7 58	
19	☙	Sexagesima Sunday	S17 22	4 03	16 28	22 40	8 25	
20	M	Baruch Spinoza d. 1677	R 7 05	4 38	17 06	23 55	8 55	
21	Tu	Rbt Southwell hanged 1595	S17 25	5 17	17 47	—	9 30	
22	W	Julie Waters b. 1950	R 7 01	6 02	18 36	1 08	10 12	
23	Th	Rotary Club founded 1905	S17 29	7 00	19 41	2 16	11 03	
24	F	Thomas Coutts d. 1822	R 6 57	8 17	20 59	3 16	12 03	
25	S	Dame Myra Hess b. 1890	S17 32	9 43	22 22	4 07	13 11	
26	☙	Quinquagesima Sunday	R 6 53	11 07	23 40	4 49	14 23	
27	M	Dame Ellen Terry b. 1848	S17 36	—	12 16	5 24	15 37	
28	Tu	Shrove Tuesday	R 6 49	0 41	13 12	5 54	16 51	

Weather column (vertical text): Cold Winter Cold, known as Buchan's great deal of sunshine. Apart from a cold spell around the 8th–16th, the month generally will be quite mild with a great deal of sunshine.

MOON'S PHASES FEBRUARY 1995

		Days	Hrs.	Mins.
☽	First Quarter	7	12	54
○	Full Moon	15	12	15
☾	Last Quarter	22	13	4

All times on this page are GMT

PREDICTIONS

February opens in the wake of the New Moon in Aquarius on January 30th. Jupiter is now in an exact square to Saturn, showing a phase of constructive growth and idealism. This also indicates that the share prices, having reached a peak, should now be facing a downward pressure. In the UK there will be expansion in the provision of education, most likely nursery education. However, there will be more cuts in education spending, suggesting that grants will be further replaced by loans. There is a high chance of inner-city riots and tension in the USA. Russia enters a critical phase relating to its Presidency, whilst internationally attention will focus on the horn of Africa, Somalia, Ethiopia and Yemen.

The Full Moon on February 15th falls in Leo, close to the Royal Star, Regulus. This suggests announcements concerning the marriage and domestic status of the Princess of Wales, perhaps a new home or relationship. There will also be speculation concerning a snap general election, and opposition and government could be very evenly balanced in the opinion polls. There could also be signs of buoyancy in the housing market. Israel and Palestine enter a phase of maximum tension lasting until mid-April, with a terrorist alert around the 13th–16th.

The Tote Gold Trophy at Newbury may be won by a horse carrying 10st 6lbs.

Published EVERY YEAR since 1697

Predicted German Reunification 1990

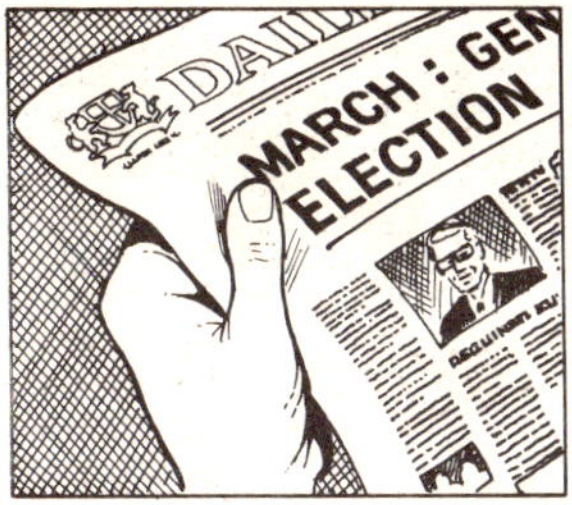

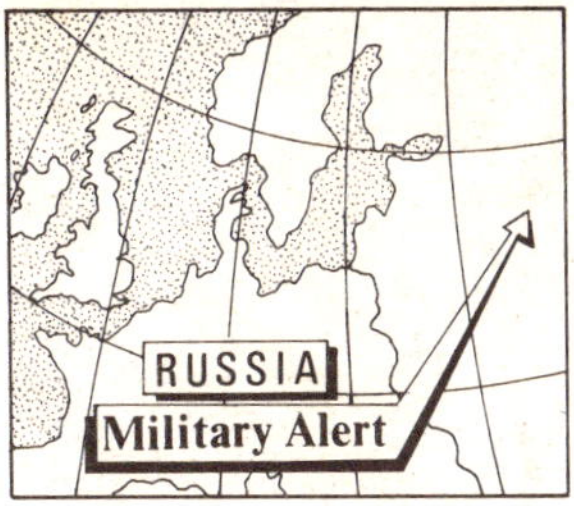

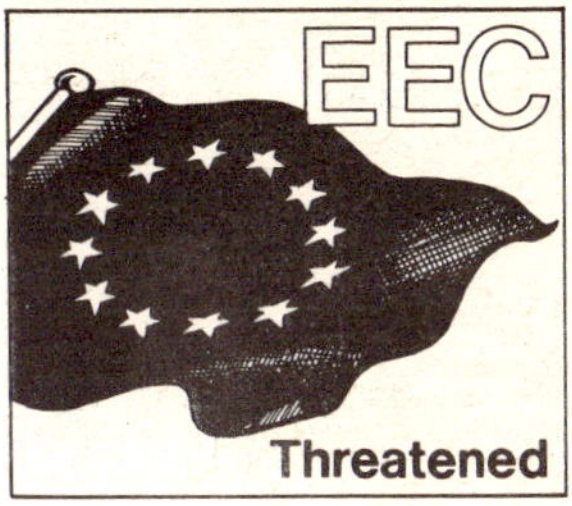

MARCH

For High Water add, for Bristol 5h. 30m., Hull 4h. 23m., Leith 0h. 43m., and for Dublin sub. 2h. 21m., Greenock 1h. 22m., Liverpool 2h. 29m.

D of M	D of W	Sundays, Festivals Special Events, etc., for 1995	Sun Rises R Sets S	High Water at London Bridge		Moon at London		Weather
				Morn.	After.	Rises	Sets	
			h. m.	h. m.	h. m.	h. m.	h. m.	
1	W	Ash Wed./St David	S17 39	1 31	13 59	6 20	18 04	We never get through March without a few very gusty days. The first half will be cold, followed by milder conditions but with strong winds and a few gales.
2	Th	Dame Naomi James b. 1949	R 6 44	2 14	14 41	6 44	19 16	
3	F	Jean Harlow b. 1911	S17 43	2 54	15 18	7 08	20 25	
4	S	Kenny Dalgleish b. 1951	R 6 40	3 29	15 53	7 32	21 32	
5	☼	1st Sunday in Lent	S17 46	4 03	16 25	7 58	22 37	
6	M	Nelson Eddy d. 1967	R 6 36	4 35	16 56	8 26	23 39	
7	Tu	Viv Richards b. 1952	S17 50	5 07	17 30	8 59	—	
8	W	Russian Revol. began 1917	R 6 31	5 45	18 08	9 36	0 38	
9	Th	Foreign Legion f'd 1831	S17 53	6 29	18 53	10 19	1 32	
10	F	Prince Edward b. 1964	R 6 27	7 24	19 49	11 09	2 20	
11	S	Johnny Appleseed d. 1847	S17 57	8 31	21 01	12 05	3 03	
12	☼	2nd Sunday in Lent	R 6 22	9 49	22 21	13 06	3 40	
13	M	Commonwealth Day	S18 00	11 07	23 34	14 12	4 13	
14	Tu	*Dresden* sunk 1915	R 6 18	—	12 05	15 22	4 42	
15	W	Jul. Caesar assass. 44 BC	S18 04	0 25	12 50	16 34	5 09	
16	Th	George Ohm, b. 1787	R 6 13	1 08	13 32	17 49	5 34	
17	F	St Patrick's Day	S18 07	1 48	14 11	19 05	6 00	
18	S	Sir Robt Walpole d. 1745	R 6 09	2 27	14 49	20 23	6 27	
19	☼	3rd Sunday in Lent	S18 11	3 04	15 27	21 41	6 57	
20	M	Burlington Arcade op. 1819	R 6 04	3 41	16 07	22 57	7 31	
21	Tu	Soviet Repub. procl. 1919	S18 14	4 21	16 48	—	8 12	
22	W	Arab League founded 1945	R 5 59	5 04	17 31	0 08	9 01	
23	Th	Joan Crawford b. 1908	S18 17	5 54	18 22	1 11	9 59	
24	F	Elizabeth I d. 1603	R 5 55	6 54	19 24	2 04	11 03	
25	S	Lady Day/The Annunciation	S18 21	8 07	20 37	2 48	12 13	
26	☼	Mothering Sunday	R 5 50	9 26	21 58	3 25	13 25	
27	M	W. von Röntgen b. 1845	S18 24	10 49	23 19	3 56	14 38	
28	Tu	Virginia Woolf d. 1941	R 5 56	11 58	—	4 22	15 49	
29	W	Royal Alb. Hall op. 1871	S18 27	0 20	12 53	4 47	17 00	
30	Th	Tom Sharpe b. 1928	R 5 41	1 11	13 39	5 11	18 09	
31	F	John Constable d. 1837	S18 31	1 53	14 19	5 34	19 17	

MOON'S PHASES MARCH 1995

		Days	*Hrs.*	*Mins.*
●	New Moon	1	11	48
☽	First Quarter	9	10	14
○	Full Moon	17	1	26
☾	Last Quarter	23	20	10
●	New Moon	31	2	9

All times GMT (BST from March 26 + 1 hour)

PREDICTIONS

The New Moon on the 1st falls in Pisces in conjunction with Saturn and a square to Jupiter. Mercury is opposed to Saturn. This will have two major consequences: firstly a sharp drop in share prices, and secondly a bout of British election fever. In the event of a snap general election being called, March is one of the key months. There could also be changes in the leadership of the Conservative Party, as well as moves to reinstate an elected government for London. The United States will be formulating a major foreign policy announcement to cope with changes in Russia and Europe. In Russia the period around the 11th brings a military alert, with the army taking a key role in both government and foreign policy, suggesting a possible coup.

The Full Moon on March 17th falls in Virgo in a trine to Uranus and Neptune. In the UK this is an inflationary pressure, suggesting that the government will still be unable to control public spending or the national debt. Serious arguments in the EEC appear to threaten its continued existence, but will pass by the end of April. China reaches its phase of maximum belligerence and may impose its own government on Hong Kong.

The Lincoln Handicap may be won by a horse carrying 8st 8lbs and the Grand National by the second favourite.

Clocks forward, 1 hour 26 March

Predicted Yeltsin's Power Struggle 1993

COMMUNISTS—POPULAR

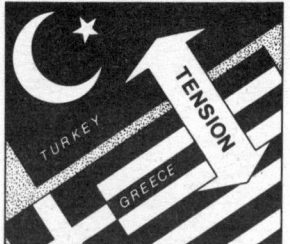

International
Negotiations

APRIL

For High Water add, for Bristol 5h. 30m., Hull 4h. 23m., Leith 0h. 43m., and for Dublin sub. 2h. 21m., Greenock 1h. 22m., Liverpool 2h. 29m.

D of M	D of W	Sundays, Festivals Special Events, etc., for 1995	Sun Rises R Sets S	High Water at London Bridge Morn.	High Water at London Bridge After.	Moon at London Rises	Moon at London Sets	Weather
			h. m.	h. m.	h. m.	h. m.	h. m.	
1	S	All Fools' Day	R 5 37	2 31	14 54	6 00	20 22	
2	☙	Passion Sunday	S18 34	3 05	15 26	6 27	21 26	
3	M	Brixton riots began 1981	R 5 32	3 36	15 54	6 58	22 26	
4	Tu	Muddy Waters b. 1915	S18 37	4 05	16 24	7 33	23 22	
5	W	Addled Parl't began 1614	R 5 28	4 39	16 55	8 14	—	of course, the
6	Th	Eden became PM 1955	S18 41	5 16	17 30	9 01	0 13	
7	F	St Francis Xavier b. 1506	R 5 23	5 56	18 11	9 54	0 57	
8	S	Tony Banks b. 1943	S18 44	6 43	18 57	10 52	1 36	weather and,
9	☙	Palm Sunday	R 5 19	7 41	19 59	11 55	2 10	
10	M	S. Hahnemann b. 1755	S18 48	8 55	21 23	13 02	2 40	sunny
11	Tu	Josephine Baker d. 1975	R 5 14	10 14	22 43	14 11	3 08	milder
12	W	F. D. Roosevelt d. 1945	S18 51	11 21	23 45	15 24	3 33	much
13	Th	J. de la Fontaine d. 1695	R 5 10	—	12 15	16 39	3 59	May flowers.
14	F	Good Friday	S18 54	0 34	13 01	17 57	4 25	that bring forth
15	S	Passover/Pesach	R 5 06	1 18	13 43	19 17	4 54	way
16	☙	Easter Day	S18 58	1 59	14 24	20 36	5 27	give
17	M	Easter Monday	R 5 01	2 40	15 05	21 52	6 06	will
18	Tu	Albert Einstein d. 1955	S19 01	3 22	15 47	23 00	6 54	showers
19	W	Primrose Day	R 4 57	4 07	16 32	23 59	7 50	April
20	Th	Alan Beith b. 1943	S19 04	4 56	17 20	—	8 54	snowy
21	F	Elizabeth II b. 1926	R 4 53	5 49	18 12	0 47	10 04	and
22	S	Kathleen Ferrier b. 1912	S19 08	6 49	19 10	1 27	11 17	start
23	☙	Low Sunday/St George	R 4 49	7 53	20 16	1 59	12 29	frosty
24	M	Anthony Trollope b. 1815	S19 11	9 05	21 30	2 27	13 40	A frosty and snowy April showers will give way that bring forth May flowers.
25	Tu	Anzac Day/St Mark	R 4 45	10 24	22 50	2 52	14 50	traditional April showers
26	W	Diet of Worms ended 1521	S19 14	11 33	23 55	3 15	15 58	
27	Th	London Zoo opened 1828	R 4 41	—	12 29	3 39	17 06	
28	F	Mussolini shot 1945	S19 17	0 47	13 14	4 03	18 11	
29	S	Zipper patent 1913	R 4 37	1 29	13 53	4 29	19 15	
30	☙	2nd Sunday after Easter	S19 21	2 07	14 28	4 58	20 17	

MOON'S PHASES APRIL 1995

			Days	Hrs.	Mins.
☽	First Quarter		8	5	35
○	Full Moon		15	12	8
☾	Last Quarter		22	3	18
●	New Moon		29	17	36

All times on this page are GMT (Add 1 hour BST)

PREDICTIONS

April opens in the wake of the New Moon in Aries on March 31st, and is in a wide trine to Mars and Jupiter indicating optimism, enthusiasm and a belief in success. Share prices will be affected by persistent downward pressure until after the 23rd, when upward pressure will be restored. In Russia the communists are likely to be increasing their popularity as part of a general world revival of socialist fortunes. In Germany the economy will be dominated by caution and contraction, implying a cut in interest rates, or even a devaluation. Italy may see changes in its government, almost certainly of the President or Prime Minister, whilst in Greece and Turkey tension reaches a peak between the 11th and 16th, with fears of war.

The Full Moon on April 15th is an eclipse and is opposed to Mercury and square to Neptune. At London Mars is rising and the Sun is culminating. Pressure builds up for a change of leader in the Labour Party. All international negotiations will be affected by a combination of idealism and muddle, with great hopes liable to flounder on self-interest. Egypt enters a phase of serious instability which lasts until September.

At Newmarket the Craven Stakes may be won by the favourite, and the Newmarket Stakes by the second favourite.

THE OLDEST ANNUAL PUBLICATION

OLD MOORE predicted the General Strike to the day — 3rd May 1926

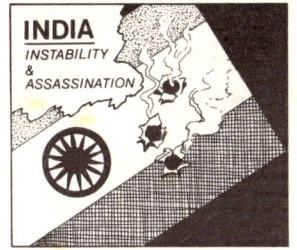

INDIA
INSTABILITY
&
ASSASSINATION

MAY

For High Water add, for Bristol 5h. 30m., Hull 4h. 23m., Leith 0h. 43m., and for Dublin sub. 2h. 21m., Greenock 1h. 22m., Liverpool 2h. 29m.

D of M	D of W	Sundays, Festivals Special Events, etc., for 1995	Sun Rises R Sets S	High Water at London Bridge Morn.	After.	Moon at London Rises	Sets	Weather
			h. m.	h. m.	h. m.	h. m.	h. m.	
1	M	Bank Holiday	R 4 33	2 40	14 58	5 32	21 14	
2	Tu	Berlin surrender 1945	S19 24	3 11	15 26	6 11	22 07	
3	W	Thomas Hood d. 1845	R 4 29	3 41	15 56	6 56	22 54	
4	Th	Cunard Co. founded 1839	S19 27	4 15	16 28	7 46	23 35	
5	F	Empress Eugénie b. 1826	R 4 26	4 52	17 03	8 42	—	
6	S	Maria Montessori d. 1952	S19 31	5 31	17 41	9 42	0 10	
7	�	3rd Sunday after Easter	R 4 24	6 15	18 23	10 46	0 41	
8	M	VE Day 1945	S19 34	7 04	19 15	11 53	1 08	
9	Tu	Lilian Baylis b. 1874	R 4 19	8 06	20 24	13 02	1 34	
10	W	Denis Thatcher b. 1915	S19 37	9 23	21 50	14 14	1 59	
11	Th	Battle of Fontenoy 1745	R 4 15	10 36	23 00	15 29	2 24	
12	F	Gabriel Fauré b. 1845	S19 40	11 38	23 58	16 47	2 51	
13	S	Daphne du Maurier b. 1907	R 4 12	—	12 30	18 07	3 21	
14	☾	4th Sunday after Easter	S19 43	0 49	13 18	19 26	3 57	
15	M	St Dympna	R 4 09	1 35	14 03	20 41	4 41	
16	Tu	Woody Herman b. 1913	S19 46	2 21	14 47	21 46	5 34	
17	W	Sandro Botticelli d. 1510	R 4 06	3 08	15 33	22 41	6 37	
18	Th	BBC founded 1922	S19 49	3 57	16 19	23 25	7 48	
19	F	James Boswell d. 1795	R 4 03	4 49	17 09	—	9 02	
20	S	Treaty of Jedda 1927	S19 52	5 41	17 59	0 01	10 17	
21	☾	Rogation Sunday	R 4 01	6 36	18 53	0 31	11 30	
22	M	Sp. Armada set sail 1588	S19 55	7 34	19 49	0 57	12 41	
23	Tu	Heinrich Himmler d. 1945	R 3 58	8 37	20 55	1 21	13 50	
24	W	Dartmoor Prison op. 1809	S19 57	9 49	22 14	1 44	14 57	
25	Th	Ascension Day	R 3 56	11 00	23 24	2 08	16 03	
26	F	Robert Morley b. 1908	S20 00	11 59	—	2 33	17 07	
27	S	Isadora Duncan b. 1878	R 3 54	0 19	12 47	3 01	18 09	
28	☾	Ascension Sunday	S20 03	1 04	13 28	3 33	19 08	
29	M	Bank Holiday	R 3 32	1 43	14 02	4 10	20 03	
30	Tu	P. C. Fabergé b. 1846	S20 05	2 17	14 33	4 52	20 52	
31	W	Islamic New Year (1416)	R 3 50	2 49	15 02	5 41	21 35	

Weather column (spanning): *After an unsettled start with cold blustery showers, the second half of the month will be much warmer, but there will be the odd thundery outburst.*

MOON'S PHASES MAY 1995

			Days	Hrs.	Mins.
☽	First Quarter		7	21	44
○	Full Moon		14	20	48
☾	Last Quarter		21	11	36
●	New Moon		29	9	27

All times on this page are GMT (Add 1 hour BST)

PREDICTIONS

May begins in the wake of the eclipsed New Moon in Taurus on April 19th. By mid-May there will be a major terrorist alert in Northern Ireland. British attention will be focused on foreign policy, with European union being a major political issue. A senior member of the Conservative Party will resign. The opposition parties will be making radical proposals, perhaps concerning closer links between the regions and Brussels, bypassing Westminster. Gains by the Liberal Democrats in the local elections will create an exaggerated impression of the party's true support. In Russia a threat to national independence suggests reunification with another ex-Soviet state. India enters a phase of instability lasting until the end of May which could see the assassination of a major political figure.

The Full Moon on May 14th falls in Scorpio in a conjunction with Pluto and a square with Mars, raising a full-scale terrorist alert. Northern Ireland should be on maximum alert, although any attacks are unlikely to diminish the push for peace. The Israeli situation will be extremely tense, although it is not unlikely that Israeli and Palestinian forces may be united against a common foe. There may be an assassination attempt on the President of Iraq.

At Newmarket the 2000 Guineas may be won by the favourite and the 1000 Guineas by the second favourite.

says the GUINNESS BOOK OF RECORDS

Predicted Oaks Winner 1993

U.S
navy active

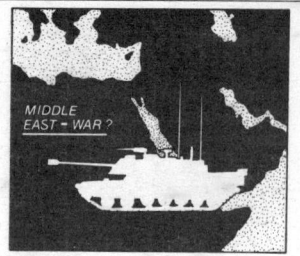

MIDDLE
EAST → WAR ?

JUNE

For High Water add, for Bristol 5h. 30m., Hull 4h. 23m.,
Leith 0h. 43m., and for Dublin sub. 2h. 21m.,
Greenock 1h. 22m., Liverpool 2h. 29m.

D of M	D of W	Sundays, Festivals Special Events, etc., for 1995	Sun Rises R Sets S	High Water at London Bridge		Moon at London		Weather
				Morn.	After.	Rises	Sets	
			h. m.	h. m.	h. m.	h. m.	h. m.	
1	Th	L-plates compulsory 1935	S20 07	3 22	15 34	6 35	22 12	
2	F	Elizabeth II crowned 1953	R 3 48	3 57	16 08	7 34	22 44	
3	S	Dunkirk evac. ended 1940	S20 09	4 34	16 43	8 36	23 12	
4	☉	Whit Sunday/Pentecost	R 3 47	5 11	17 20	9 40	23 38	
5	M	Suez Canal reopened 1975	S20 11	5 51	17 58	10 47	—	
6	Tu	Bjorn Borg b. 1956	R 3 45	6 36	18 43	11 56	0 02	
7	W	*Lusitania* launched 1906	S20 13	7 29	19 42	13 08	0 26	
8	Th	Muhammad d. 632	R 3 44	8 37	20 59	14 22	0 51	
9	F	Jan van Eyck b. 1441	S20 15	9 53	22 17	15 39	1 18	
10	S	Prince Philip b. 1921	R 3 44	11 02	23 24	16 57	1 50	
11	☉	Trinity Sunday	S20 16	—	12 02	18 14	2 29	
12	M	Thomas Arnold d. 1842	R 3 43	0 23	12 56	19 25	3 17	
13	Tu	Thomas Arnold b. 1795	S20 18	1 17	13 45	20 27	4 15	
14	W	Battle of Naseby 1645	S20 19	2 09	14 33	21 18	5 23	
15	Th	Corpus Christi	S20 19	2 58	15 20	21 59	6 38	
16	F	James Bolam b. 1938	R 3 42	3 47	16 08	22 32	7 56	
17	S	Ken Livingstone b. 1945	S20 20	4 36	16 55	23 01	9 12	
18	☉	1st Sunday after Trinity	R 3 42	5 26	17 41	23 26	10 27	
19	M	Kiel Canal opened 1895	S20 20	6 15	18 29	23 50	11 38	
20	Tu	Duchess of Glos b. 1946	R 3 42	7 05	19 19	—	12 48	
21	W	Prince William b. 1982	S20 21	8 00	20 17	0 14	13 54	
22	Th	B. of Okinawa ended 1945	R 3 43	9 04	21 26	0 38	14 59	
23	F	Empress Joséphine b. 1763	S20 21	10 17	22 45	1 05	16 02	
24	S	Lucrezia Borgia d. 1519	R 3 43	11 24	23 49	1 35	17 02	
25	☉	2nd Sunday after Trinity	S20 21	—	12 18	2 10	17 58	
26	M	UN Charter signed 1945	R 3 44	0 39	13 00	2 51	18 49	
27	Tu	Allies t'k Cherbourg 1944	S20 21	1 19	13 38	3 37	19 34	
28	W	L. Pirandello b. 1867	R 3 45	1 56	14 11	4 29	20 14	
29	Th	Rubens b. 1577/St Peter	S20 21	2 30	14 44	5 27	20 48	
30	F	Montezuma killed 1520	R 3 46	3 05	15 19	6 28	21 17	

Weather column (vertical): A showery and rather cool start will be followed by a heatwave around the middle of the month. Occasional thunderstorms can be expected towards the end.

PREDICTIONS

June begins in the wake of the New Moon in Gemini on May 29th. This brings further liberalisation in airline regulations and in TV and radio licensing. In the UK there is likely to be a dispute between the House of Commons and the House of Lords, perhaps over child care, educational matters and the arts. There is a very real chance of a significant change to the 1992 agreements incorporating Northern Ireland into the UK. The US navy may also be active, possibly within Russia itself.

The Full Moon on June 13th falls in Sagittarius and is in a square to Saturn. There could be a change of government in Brazil, but also news of rapid economic growth. *The New Moon on June 28th falls in Cancer* highlighting vital peace negotiations. Russia will be setting up a new military and security system to replace the Warsaw Pact. Russia could also be in dispute with Japan. In the Middle East there will be renewed fears of all out war, most likely as a result of Israeli nuclear threats, possibly because of the imminent fear of a political assassination in Egypt. This danger peaks in mid-July and continues until late August.

The Epsom Derby may be won by the favourite and the Oaks by a French-trained filly.

MOON'S PHASES JUNE 1995			Days	Hrs.	Mins.
☽	First Quarter		6	10	26
○	Full Moon		13	4	3
☾	Last Quarter		19	22	1
●	New Moon		28	0	50

All times on this page are GMT (Add 1 hour BST)

Mail a copy of FOULSHAM'S ALMANACK to your friends abroad

Predicted the abidication of King Edward VIII 1936

JULY

For High Water add, for Bristol 5h. 30m., Hull 4h. 23m., Leith 0h. 43m., and for Dublin sub. 2h. 21m., Greenock 1h. 22m., Liverpool 2h. 29m.

D of M	D of W	Sundays, Festivals Special Events, etc., for 1995	Sun Rises R Sets S	High Water at London Bridge Morn.	High Water at London Bridge After.	Moon at London Rises	Moon at London Sets	Wea-ther
			h. m.	h. m.	h. m.	h. m.	h. m.	
1	S	Princess of Wales b. 1961	S20 20	3 41	15 54	7 32	21 44	
2	☀	3rd Sunday after Trinity	R 3 47	4 17	16 28	8 38	22 08	
3	M	Battle of Santiago 1898	S20 20	4 53	17 02	9 45	22 32	
4	Tu	US Independence Day	R 3 49	5 30	17 37	10 54	22 56	
5	W	Sarah Siddons b. 1755	S20 19	6 09	18 16	12 06	23 21	
6	Th	USSR constituted 1923	R 3 51	6 57	19 07	13 19	—	
7	F	St Cyril & St Methodius	S20 18	7 57	20 19	14 34	0 24	
8	S	Christian Huygens d. 1695	R 3 52	9 13	21 40	15 49	1 05	
9	☀	4th Sunday after Trinity	S20 16	10 29	22 57	17 02	1 56	
10	M	John Calvin b. 1509	R 3 54	11 38	—	18 08	2 59	
11	Tu	Alfred Dryfus d. 1935	S20 15	0 06	12 39	19 04	4 10	
12	W	Bank Holiday (NI)	R 3 56	1 05	13 34	19 51	5 27	
13	Th	Sir Alec Rose b. 1908	S20 13	1 59	14 21	20 29	6 46	
14	F	National day of France	R 3 59	2 48	15 08	21 01	8 04	
15	S	St Swithun's Day	S20 11	3 34	15 53	21 29	9 19	
16	☀	5th Sunday after Trinity	R 4 01	4 21	16 35	21 54	10 31	
17	M	Postdam Conf. began 1945	S20 09	5 04	17 17	22 18	11 41	
18	Tu	Jane Austen d. 1817	R 4 03	5 48	17 59	22 43	12 48	
19	W	*Mary Rose* sank 1545	S20 07	6 32	18 44	23 09	13 52	
20	Th	Jacques Delors b. 1925	R 4 06	7 19	19 35	23 38	14 54	
21	F	Maraquesas Is discov. 1595	S20 05	8 14	20 37	—	15 51	
22	S	Florenz Ziegfeld d. 1932	R 4 09	9 19	21 51	0 12	16 44	
23	☀	6th Sunday after Trinity	S20 02	10 36	23 14	0 50	17 32	
24	M	Robert Graves b. 1895	R 4 11	11 44	—	1 34	18 13	
25	Tu	Blériot flew Channel 1909	S19 59	0 12	12 33	2 24	18 50	
26	W	Moll Cutpurse d. 1659	R 4 14	0 56	13 12	3 20	19 21	
27	Th	B. of Killiecrankie 1689	S19 57	1 34	13 48	4 20	19 49	
28	F	J. S. Bach d. 1750	R 4 17	2 10	14 26	5 23	20 15	
29	S	Treaty of Moscow 1945	S19 54	2 45	15 01	6 29	20 39	
30	☀	7th Sunday after Trinity	R 4 20	3 22	15 36	7 37	21 02	
31	M	Evonne Cawley b. 1951	S19 50	3 57	16 08	8 45		

On average July is the hottest month of the summer and a heatwave around mid-month sees temperatures of over 80°F. But watch out for a spot of thunder towards the end.

MOON'S PHASES JULY 1995

		Days	Hrs.	Mins.
☽	First Quarter	5	20	2
○	Full Moon	12	20	49
☾	Last Quarter	19	11	10
●	New Moon	27	15	13

All times on this page are GMT (Add 1 hour BST)

PREDICTIONS

The Full Moon on July 12th falls in Cancer in a square to the UK Moon, denoting a rash of news stories concerning 'women's issues', especially the need for the government, House of Commons and legal system to include more women. Mars is in opposition to Saturn indicating global tension, but conflict should be avoided. In Russia there will be ministerial changes in the government. There will again be troop movements in Greece and Turkey, with fears of war. There could be the threat of a military coup in Turkey. In Italy political violence could also raise concerns over army intervention in government.

The New Moon on July 27th falls in Leo in a conjunction with Mercury, sextile to Mars and trine to Jupiter, indicating a general mood of optimism and willingness to reach agreement. There could even be a sense of euphoria that long-running global disputes are about to be settled. *In the UK Pluto is rising in trine to Saturn* indicating that there may be a scandal connecting the opposition to a criminal figure. Italy now enters a period of fundamental constitutional change, when the existence of the state will be called into question. However, all the indications are that the issue will be deferred.

At Goodwood Races the Stewards Cup may be won by the top weight. Favourites may be worth following in the non-handicaps.

1996 OLD MOORE on sale July 1995

LIBERALISATION
OF AIRWAYS

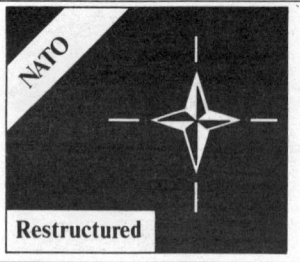

Restructured

AUGUST

For High Water add, for Bristol 5h. 30m., Hull 4h. 23m., Leith 0h. 43m., and for Dublin sub. 2h. 21m., Greenock 1h. 22m., Liverpool 2h. 29m.

D of M	D of W	Sundays, Festivals Special Events, etc., for 1995	Sun Rises R Sets S	High Water at London Bridge Morn.	High Water at London Bridge After.	Moon at London Rises	Moon at London Sets	Weather
			h. m.	h. m.	h. m.	h. m.	h. m.	
1	Tu	London Bridge opened 1831	R 4 23	4 32	16 41	9 56	21 27	
2	W	Potsdam Conf. ended 1945	S19 47	5 07	17 16	11 07	21 54	
3	Th	Hudson Bay discov'd 1610	R 4 26	5 44	17 54	12 20	22 25	
4	F	Queen Mother b. 1900	S19 44	6 29	18 41	13 33	23 03	
5	S	Marilyn Monroe d. 1962	R 4 29	7 25	19 49	14 45	23 48	
6	☻	8th Sunday after Trinity	S19 40	8 41	21 15	15 52	—	
7	M	Bank Holiday (Scot.)	R 4 32	10 01	22 39	16 51	0 43	
8	Tu	Hiroshima A-bomb 1945	S19 37	11 19	23 55	17 41	1 48	
9	W	Nagasaki A-bomb 1945	R 4 35	—	12 25	18 23	3 01	
10	Th	Treaty of Sévres 1920	S19 33	0 57	13 21	18 58	4 19	
11	F	First Ascot races 1711	R 4 38	1 49	14 09	19 28	5 37	
12	S	US annexed Hawaii 1898	S19 29	2 35	14 52	19 55	6 54	
13	☻	9th Sunday after Trinity	R 4 41	3 19	15 33	20 20	8 09	
14	M	Japanese surrender 1945	S19 25	4 00	16 12	20 46	9 21	
15	Tu	Princess Royal b. 1950	R 4 45	4 39	16 50	21 12	10 31	
16	W	Battle of the Spurs 1513	S19 21	5 17	17 27	21 41	11 38	
17	Th	Indonesia independent 1945	R 4 48	5 55	18 06	22 12	12 41	
18	F	Shelley Winters b. 1922	S19 17	6 36	18 54	22 49	13 41	
19	S	James Watt d. 1819	R 4 51	7 25	19 52	23 31	14 36	
20	☻	10th Sunday after Trinity	S19 13	8 26	21 01	—	15 26	
21	M	Princess Margaret b. 1930	R 4 54	9 36	22 25	0 18	16 10	
22	Tu	Red Cross founded 1864	S19 09	11 02	23 41	1 11	16 48	
23	W	Visigoths sacked Rome 410	R 4 57	—	12 02	2 10	17 22	
24	Th	Col. Thos Blood d. 1680	S19 05	0 29	12 46	3 12	17 52	
25	F	Pliny the Elder d. 79	R 5 00	1 08	13 24	4 18	18 18	
26	S	US women's suffrage 1920	S19 01	1 45	14 00	5 25	18 43	
27	☻	11th Sunday after Trinity	R 5 04	2 21	14 37	6 35	19 08	
28	M	Bank Holiday (not Scot.)	S18 56	2 56	15 11	7 45	19 33	
29	Tu	The Ashes instituted 1882	R 5 07	3 33	15 44	8 57	20 00	
30	W	Leningrad siege b'n 1941	S18 52	4 08	16 19	10 10	20 30	
31	Th	Edwin Moses b. 1955	R 5 10	4 43	16 55	11 23	21 05	

The good weather continues with temperatures reaching 80°F. Very warm and sunny with just the occasional thunderstorm. Outbreaks of rain towards the latter part.

MOON'S PHASES AUGUST 1995		Days	Hrs.	Mins.
☽ First Quarter		4	3	16
○ Full Moon		10	18	16
☾ Last Quarter		18	3	4
● New Moon		26	4	31

All times on this page are GMT (Add 1 hour BST)

PREDICTIONS

The Full Moon on the 10th falls in Aquarius in a trine to Mars. Through the UK and central Europe Pluto is culminating and Uranus and Neptune are rising revealing that minor political events could have a dramatic historic significance. The EEC budget will be rising, but arguments will concern the rapidly rising cost of plans for European Union. There are now excellent chances of a settlement to the Bosnian crisis, at least in the medium term, and the easing of planetary pressures in the Balkans indicates that the worst of the crisis is now over. Germany will be taking a lead in European foreign policy, and will be exerting a veto over the actions of the European parliament and commission.

The New Moon on the 26th falls in Virgo and is in a square to Jupiter. Saturn is opposed to Mercury indicating serious financial muddles in the UK, most likely massive wastage of funds in the health service. There are signs of complete reorganisation in the airline industry, with liberalisation of the airways. NATO will be radically restructuring its membership, though the admission of new members is less likely than the reaching of bilateral defence agreements with individual states. The effect though, will be to expand the NATO military block. There is the possibility of political riots in India.

At York Races the Ebor Handicap may be won by a 5-y-o carrying 8st 8lbs, and the Great Voltigeur Stakes by the second favourite.

Something for Everyone in MOORE'S ALMANACK

Predicted St Leger Winner 1993

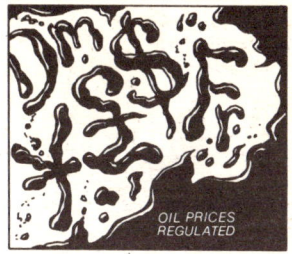

OIL PRICES REGULATED

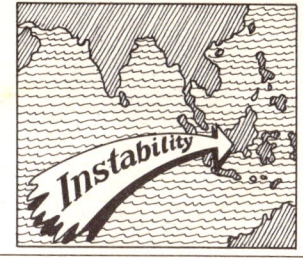

SEPTEMBER

For High Water add, for Bristol 5h. 30m., Hull 4h. 23m.,
Leith 0h. 43m., and for Dublin sub. 2h. 21m.,
Greenock 1h. 22m., Liverpool 2h. 29m.

D of M	D of W	Sundays, Festivals Special Events, etc., for 1995	Sun Rises R Sets S	High Water at London Bridge Morn.	High Water at London Bridge After.	Moon at London Rises	Moon at London Sets	Wea- ther
			h. m.	h. m.	h. m.	h. m.	h. m.	
1	F	Cecil Parkinson b. 1931	S18 48	5 21	17 35	12 34	21 47	
2	S	Jap. surrender signed 1945	R 5 13	6 05	18 26	13 41	22 37	
3	☉	12th Sunday after Trinity	S18 43	7 01	19 35	14 42	23 37	
4	M	Anton Bruckner b. 1824	R 5 16	8 17	21 01	15 34	—	
5	Tu	Catherine Parr d. 1548	S18 39	9 40	22 26	16 18	0 45	
6	W	*Mayflower* set sail 1620	R 5 20	11 02	23 42	16 55	1 58	
7	Th	London Blitz began 1940	S18 34	—	12 11	17 26	3 14	
8	F	Treaty of Portsmouth 1819	R 5 23	0 43	13 05	17 55	4 30	
9	S	Wm the Conqueror d. 1087	S18 30	1 35	13 52	18 21	5 46	
10	☉	13th Sunday after Trinity	R 5 26	2 19	14 33	18 47	6 59	
11	M	FA Cup stolen 1895	S18 25	2 59	15 11	19 13	8 11	
12	Tu	Hudson R. discov'd 1609	R 5 29	3 36	15 47	19 41	9 20	
13	W	Clara Schumann b. 1819	S18 18	4 11	16 22	20 12	10 25	
14	Th	Dante d. 1321	R 5 32	4 43	16 56	20 47	11 28	
15	F	Beirut civil war b'n 1975	S18 16	5 17	17 33	21 27	12 25	
16	S	Lake Nyasa discov'd 1859	R 5 35	5 54	18 15	22 12	13 17	
17	☉	14th Sunday after Trinity	S18 11	6 37	19 08	23 03	14 04	
18	M	Greta Garbo b. 1905	R 5 39	7 34	20 16	23 59	14 44	
19	Tu	Siege of Paris began 1870	S18 07	8 45	21 33	—	15 20	
20	W	P. de Sarasate d. 1908	R 5 42	10 07	22 55	0 59	15 51	
21	Th	B. of Prestonpans 1745	S18 02	11 21	23 52	2 03	16 19	
22	F	Gen. Perón deposed 1955	R 5 45	—	12 12	3 09	16 45	
23	S	Augustus Caesar b. 63 BC	S17 57	0 36	12 53	4 18	17 10	
24	☉	15th Sunday after Trinity	R 5 48	1 15	13 31	5 29	17 36	
25	M	Jewish New Year (5756)	S17 53	1 52	14 07	6 42	18 02	
26	Tu	Béla Bartók d. 1945	R 5 52	2 30	14 44	7 56	18 32	
27	W	Adelina Patti d. 1919	S17 48	3 06	15 20	9 11	19 06	
28	Th	Louis Pasteur d. 1895	R 5 55	3 44	15 58	10 24	19 47	
29	F	St Michael & All Angels	S17 44	4 22	16 39	11 34	20 35	
30	S	Munich Agreement 1938	R 5 58	5 03	17 26	12 36	21 32	

A sunny and pleasantly warm start to the month will be followed by traditional Autumnal gales around 20th-23rd. Spells of heavy rain towards the latter part.

MOON'S PHASES SEPTEMBER 1995			Days	Hrs.	Mins.
	☽	First Quarter	2	9	3
	○	Full Moon	9	3	37
	☾	Last Quarter	16	21	9
	●	New Moon	24	16	55

All times on this page are GMT (Add 1 hour BST)

PREDICTIONS

The Full Moon on the 9th falls in Pisces in a conjunction with Saturn and an opposition to Venus, indicating concern over the high cost of the welfare state, mainly the health budget, but also child allowances, which will soon be cut or made selective. There will be serious attempts to regulate the world oil price, but any agreement is unlikely to last beyond the end of the year. Iraq completes a five month period of political restructuring, which may bring Kurdish independence closer. Renewed threats of a political assassination in India continues until mid-October.

The New Moon on the 24th falls in Libra. Venus in sextile with Jupiter indicates high hopes of peace, though agreements reached between the 22nd and 30th are unlikely to succeed. Agreements concerning the UK are most likely to be financial, and could include a row over the trade in re-processed Plutonium: the government will come under pressure to close an atomic reprocessing plant, which would be seen as a major political climb down and an economic loss. In Egypt, although instability eases temporarily, the government should keep up its guard against both street protests and the threat of political assassination. Indonesia enters a phase of instability which lasts until late November and could bring large street protests and a change of government.

At Doncaster races the St. Leger may be won by the second favourite and the Doncaster Cup by the favourite.

1996 RAPHAEL'S ASTROLOGICAL ALMANAC on sale September 1995

Predicted Disintegration of Yugoslavia 1992

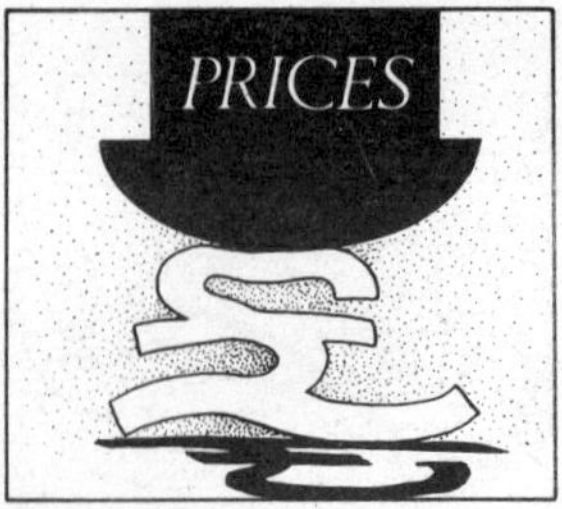

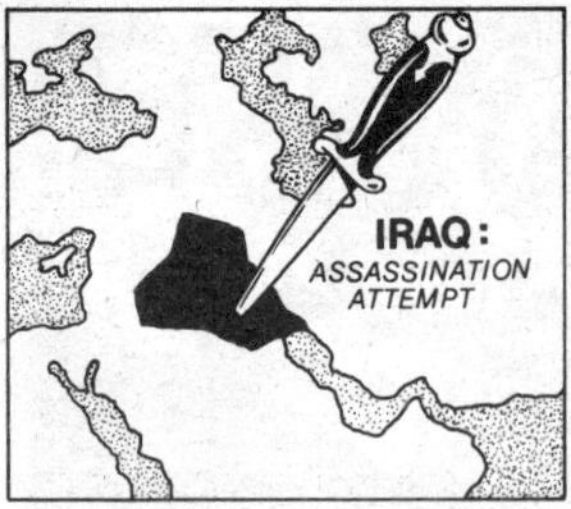

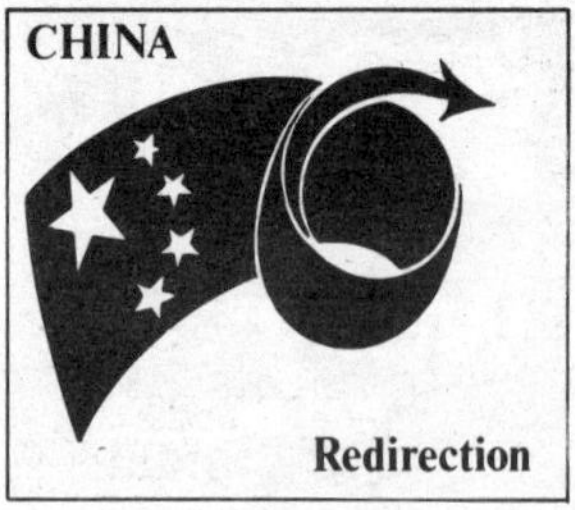

OCTOBER

For High Water add, for Bristol 5h. 30m., Hull 4h. 23m., Leith 0h. 43m., and for Dublin sub. 2h. 21m., Greenock 1h. 22m., Liverpool 2h. 29m.

D of M	D of W	Sundays, Festivals Special Events, etc., for 1995	Sun Rises R Sets S	High Water at London Bridge Morn.	High Water at London Bridge After.	Moon at London Rises	Moon at London Sets	Weather
			h. m.	h. m.	h. m.	h. m.	h. m.	
1	S	16th Sunday after Trinity	S17 39	5 51	18 20	13 13	22 36	Generally reasonably sunny and mild, particularly between the 10th–25th (St Luke's Little Summer). During the last week it will become colder with slight frosts.
2	M	Richard III b. 1452	R 6 01	6 49	19 29	14 16	23 47	
3	Tu	Eleanor Duse b. 1859	S17 34	8 00	20 49	14 55	—	
4	W	Yom Kippur	R 6 05	9 20	22 11	15 27	1 00	
5	Th	J. Offenbach d. 1880	S17 30	10 42	23 26	15 56	2 14	
6	F	Prom. Concerts f'd 1895	R 6 08	11 51	—	16 22	3 28	
7	S	Clive James b. 1939	S17 25	0 25	12 46	16 48	4 41	
8	S	17th Sunday after Trinity	R 6 11	1 15	13 32	17 13	5 52	
9	M	1st day of Tabernacles	S17 21	1 57	14 11	17 41	7 02	
10	Tu	Tyne Bridge opened 1930	R 6 15	2 35	14 48	18 11	8 09	
11	W	James Prior b. 1927	S17 17	3 11	15 22	18 44	9 13	
12	Th	Elizabeth Fry d. 1845	R 6 18	3 41	15 54	19 22	10 13	
13	F	Lady Thatcher b. 1925	S17 12	4 12	16 26	20 05	11 08	
14	S	King Harold slain 1066	R 6 21	4 42	17 03	20 54	11 57	
15	S	18th Sunday after Trinity	S17 08	5 17	17 42	21 48	12 40	
16	M	Girton College op. 1869	R 6 25	5 56	18 30	22 46	13 17	
17	Tu	Jean Arthur b. 1908	S17 04	6 44	19 28	23 47	13 50	
18	W	St Luke	R 6 28	7 46	20 41	—	14 19	
19	Th	Jonathan Swift d. 1745	S16 59	9 09	21 57	0 51	14 45	
20	F	B. of Salamis 480 BC	R 6 32	10 28	23 03	1 58	15 10	
21	S	Trafalgar Day	S16 55	11 27	23 56	3 08	15 35	
22	S	19th Sunday after Trinity	R 6 35	—	12 15	4 20	16 02	
23	M	W. G. Grace d. 1915	S16 51	0 41	12 58	5 34	16 30	
24	Tu	St Raphael the Archangel	R 6 38	1 22	13 39	6 50	17 03	
25	W	Geoffrey Chaucer d. 1400	S16 47	2 03	14 19	8 07	17 42	
26	Th	Hillary Clinton b. 1947	R 6 42	2 42	14 59	9 20	18 29	
27	F	Theo. Roosevelt b. 1858	S16 43	3 23	15 43	10 28	19 24	
28	S	Alfred the Great d. 901	R 6 46	4 05	16 29	11 27	20 28	
29	S	20th Sunday after Trinity	S16 40	4 52	17 20	12 16	21 38	
30	M	R. B. Sheridan b. 1751	R 6 49	5 42	18 18	12 56	22 50	
31	Tu	Hallowe'en	S16 36	6 39	19 21	13 30	—	

MOON'S PHASES OCTOBER 1995

		Days	Hrs.	Mins.
☽	First Quarter	1	14	36
○	Full Moon	8	15	52
☾	Last Quarter	16	16	26
●	New Moon	24	4	36
☽	First Quarter	30	21	17

All times GMT (BST to Oct 22 + 1 hr)

PREDICTIONS

The Full Moon on the 8th is an eclipse in opposition to Mercury and a trine to Jupiter. Venus is squared Uranus, indicating the breakdown of peace agreements, including those in the Balkans. Share prices should be rising up to the Mars Pluto conjunction on the 19th, after which downward pressure on prices begins, although a sharp fall may be delayed until after November 11th. There will be a major risk of terrorist attacks around the 19th, with a red alert in Israel, where a Palestinian leader may be the target. In Northern Ireland there is a last chance of a major constitutional settlement, and if peace is not achieved now, the next chance might not come until 1999. There will be an assassination attempt on the Iraqi leader.

The New Moon on the 24th is an eclipse and is sextile Mars and Pluto. Venus is in a trine to Saturn. In the UK education expenditure will be increasing. Long-term international tension is likely to be felt from Iran through the Indian sub-continent and Southeast Asia. The EEC will be introducing rules standardising transport policy and will begin to investigate the standardisation of educational policy and school vocational qualifications. China is now approaching a fundamental redirection of political and economic policy, with changes in the government.

At Newmarket races the Cambridgeshire may be won by a horse carrying 7st 13lbs, and the Cesarewitch by the favourite.

Clocks back 1 hour, 22 October

Predicted November Handicap Winner 1993

ECONOMIC GROWTH

STORMS

NOVEMBER

For High Water add, for Bristol 5h. 30m., Hull 4h. 23m., Leith 0h. 43m., and for Dublin sub. 2h. 21m., Greenock 1h. 22m., Liverpool 2h. 29m.

D of M	D of W	Sundays, Festivals Special Events, etc., for 1995	Sun Rises R Sets S	High Water at London Bridge Morn.	High Water at London Bridge After.	Moon at London Rises	Moon at London Sets	Wea-ther
			h. m.	h. m.	h. m.	h. m.	h. m.	
1	W	Congress of Vienna 1814	R 6 53	7 45	20 31	14 00	0 04	
2	Th	Marie Antoinette b. 1755	S16 32	8 56	21 47	14 26	1 17	
3	F	Karl Baedeker b. 1801	R 6 56	10 15	23 00	14 51	2 29	
4	S	Admiral J. Benbow d. 1702	S16 29	11 26	—	15 16	3 39	
5	☙	21st Sunday after Trinity	R 7 00	0 02	12 22	15 42	4 48	
6	M	Nigel Havers b. 1949	S16 25	0 53	13 10	16 11	5 55	
7	Tu	Suez cease-fire 1956	R 7 03	1 35	13 50	16 42	7 01	
8	W	X-rays discovered 1895	S16 22	2 13	14 26	17 18	8 02	
9	Th	Kaiser Wm II abdic. 1918	R 7 07	2 45	14 58	18 00	9 00	
10	F	Richard Burton b. 1925	S16 19	3 15	15 30	18 46	9 51	
11	S	Jerome Kern d. 1945	R 7 10	3 44	16 03	19 38	10 36	
12	☙	Remembrance Sunday	S16 16	4 15	16 39	20 34	11 16	
13	M	Edward III b. 1312	R 7 14	4 49	17 17	21 34	11 50	
14	Tu	Prince of Wales b. 1948	S16 13	5 27	18 01	22 36	12 20	
15	W	Cath. of Braganza b. 1638	R 7 17	6 09	18 47	23 40	12 47	
16	Th	Paul Hindemith b. 1895	S16 10	6 57	19 46	—	13 11	
17	F	H. Villa-Lobos d. 1959	R 7 21	8 03	20 59	0 47	13 36	
18	S	Marcel Proust d. 1922	S16 07	9 26	22 11	1 56	14 01	
19	☙	23rd Sunday after Trinity	R 7 24	10 36	23 13	3 08	14 27	
20	M	Battle of Cambrai 1917	S16 05	11 35	—	4 23	14 57	
21	Tu	Henry Purcell d. 1695	R 7 27	0 06	12 26	5 40	15 33	
22	W	George Eliot b. 1819	S16 03	0 56	13 12	6 56	16 16	
23	Th	Thomas Tallis d. 1585	R 7 30	1 41	13 59	8 09	17 09	
24	F	Billy Connolly b. 1942	S16 01	2 24	14 44	9 14	18 11	
25	S	Francis Durbridge b. 1912	R 7 34	3 08	15 32	10 10	19 22	
26	☙	24th Sunday after Trinity	S15 59	3 54	16 21	10 55	20 36	
27	M	Ernie Wise b. 1925	R 7 37	4 42	17 13	11 33	21 52	
28	Tu	Royal Soc. founded 1660	S15 57	5 33	18 08	12 04	23 07	
29	W	Louisa M. Alcott b. 1832	R 7 40	6 25	19 05	12 32	—	
30	Th	St Andrew's Day	S15 56	7 22	20 07	12 57	0 19	

Some pleasant sunny days, but a sharp drop in temperature during the month with keen night frosts and we will see the first snow showers of winter.

MOON'S PHASES NOVEMBER 1995

			Days	Hrs.	Mins.
○	Full Moon		7	7	21
☾	Last Quarter		15	11	40
●	New Moon		22	15	43
☽	First Quarter		29	6	28

All times on this page are GMT

PREDICTIONS

The Full Moon on the 7th is in Taurus. Mars will be in conjunction with Jupiter indicating increasing government expenditure. The Conservative Party will be subject to substantial reorganisation, perhaps a new chairman and a democratisation of its structure. There is also now a ninety per cent chance of a leadership contest in the Labour Party. Support for Labour will be growing and the Trades Unions will reinforce their support for the leadership. There could be storms on the eastern US seaboard, with Florida being particularly exposed. The USA will be in an expansive and aggressive mood, and US troops will almost certainly be in action overseas between the 10th and 19th. In Russia there will be massive shows of opposition to the government. In Germany economic growth will be dramatic and we may see the informal creation of a 'deutschmark' zone with currencies in Eastern Europe as well as west shadowing the Germany currency. *The New Moon on the 22nd will fall in Scorpio, conjunct Mercury and Pluto,* indicating very difficult negotiations between the British government and its partners over trade, travel and nuclear issues, probably complicated by allegations about nuclear waste and corruption. *Venus, Mars and Jupiter will be in a conjunction on the 8th cusp at London,* indicating a giveaway budget with spending and tax concessions designed to create a mood of prosperity.

At Doncaster races the November Handicap may be won by the favourite.

OLD MOORE'S predictions are world famous

Predicted King George VI Chase Winner 1993

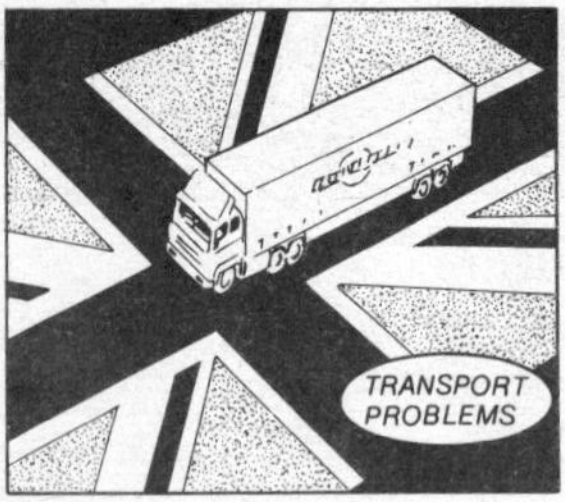

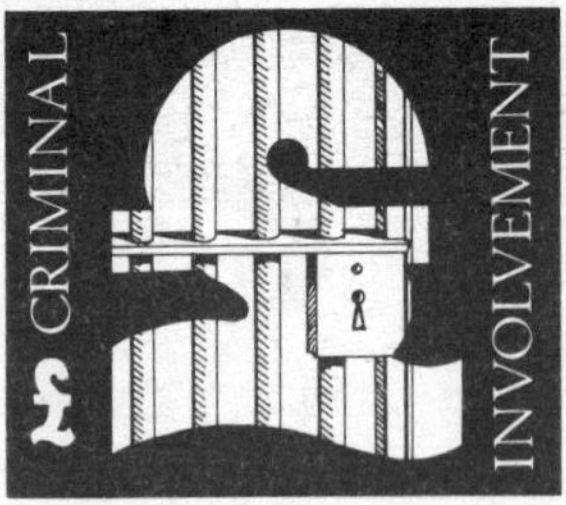

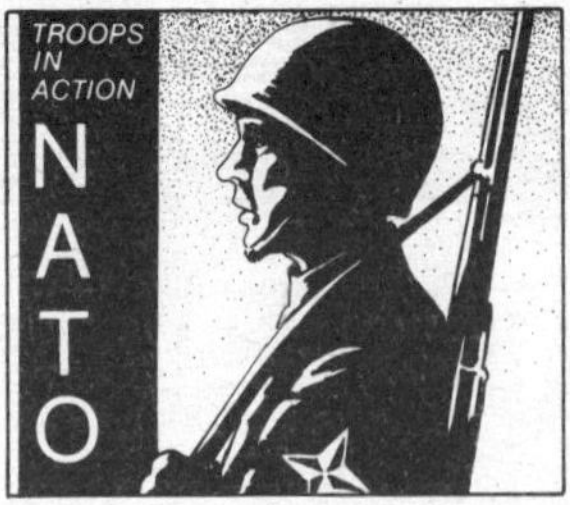

DECEMBER

For High Water add, for Bristol 5h. 30m., Hull 4h. 23m., Leith 0h. 43m., and for Dublin sub. 2h. 21m., Greenock 1h. 22m., Liverpool 2h. 29m.

D of M	D of W	Sundays, Festivals Special Events, etc., for 1995	Sun Rises R Sets S	High Water at London Bridge Morn.	High Water at London Bridge After.	Moon at London Rises	Moon at London Sets	Weather
			h. m.	h. m.	h. m.	h. m.	h. m.	
1	F	Henry I d. 1135	R 7 43	8 26	21 15	13 22	1 30	Very cold and wintry spells will occur shortly before Christmas and again after. The rest of the month will be a mixture of very changeable weather.
2	S	Marquis de Sade d. 1814	S15 54	9 40	22 29	13 47	2 39	
3	S	1st Sunday in Advent	R 7 45	10 55	23 34	14 14	3 46	
4	M	Thomas Carlyle b. 1795	S15 53	11 56	—	14 44	4 51	
5	Tu	Prohibition repeal 1933	R 7 48	0 27	12 46	15 18	5 54	
6	W	Battle of Cawnpore 1857	S15 52	1 11	13 28	15 56	6 52	
7	Th	Ellen Burstyn b. 1932	R 7 50	1 49	14 06	16 41	7 46	
8	F	Sammy Davis, Jr b. 1925	S15 52	2 23	14 38	17 31	8 34	
9	S	Danny Blanchflower d. 1993	R 7 53	2 54	15 12	18 25	9 16	
10	S	2nd Sunday in Advent	S15 51	3 23	15 46	19 24	9 52	
11	M	George VI accession 1936	R 7 55	3 57	16 21	20 25	10 23	
12	Tu	Douglas Firbanks d. 1939	S15 51	4 31	16 57	21 28	10 50	
13	W	Council of Trent b'n 1545	R 7 57	5 06	17 35	22 32	11 16	
14	Th	George VI b. 1895	S15 51	5 42	18 16	23 38	11 39	
15	F	B. of Kesselsdorf 1745	R 7 59	6 23	19 04	—	12 03	
16	S	Jane Austen b. 1775	S15 51	7 14	20 04	0 47	12 28	
17	S	3rd Sunday in Advent	R 8 00	8 23	21 19	1 58	12 55	
18	M	B. of Clifton Moor 1745	S15 52	9 46	22 31	3 11	13 26	
19	Tu	Vitus Bering d. 1741	R 8 02	10 56	23 34	4 27	14 04	
20	W	Irene Dunne b. 1904	S15 52	11 58	—	5 41	14 51	
21	Th	Gen. Geo. Patton d. 1945	R 8 03	0 30	12 53	6 52	15 48	
22	F	Noel Edmonds b. 1948	S15 53	1 22	13 45	7 54	16 56	
23	S	J. Arthur Rank b. 1888	R 8 04	2 10	14 34	8 47	18 11	
24	S	Christmas Eve	S15 54	2 56	15 23	9 30	19 29	
25	M	Christmas Day	R 8 05	3 43	16 12	10 05	20 48	
26	Tu	Boxing Day	S15 56	4 31	17 00	10 35	22 04	
27	W	Methuen Treaty 1703	R 8 05	5 17	17 49	11 02	23 18	
28	Th	Tay Bridge collapse 1879	S15 57	6 05	18 40	11 28	—	
29	F	Jameson Raid 1895	R 8 06	6 54	19 35	11 53	0 29	
30	S	Richard Rodgers d. 1979	S15 59	7 50	20 35	12 19	1 37	
31	S	New Year's Eve	R 8 06	8 56	21 46	12 48	2 43	

MOON'S PHASES DECEMBER 1995

		Days	*Hrs.*	*Mins.*
○	Full Moon	7	1	27
☾	Last Quarter	15	5	31
●	New Moon	22	2	22
☽	First Quarter	28	19	6

All times on this page are GMT

PREDICTIONS

The Full Moon on the 7th falls in Gemini in a square to Saturn. In the UK there could be transport problems, including a spate of mechanical failures, but also industrial action by rail or airline staff. University teachers may also be talking of strike action. All pressures in Serbia should now have eased, indicating that the Balkan problem will now be open to a long-term solution.

The New Moon this month falls on the 22nd and is conjunct Jupiter and the galactic centre, indicating that even apparently trivial events may come to have a major global significance, affecting the world balance of power. Events in Russia, China and the USA over the coming two or three months should be seen in this light. In the UK there will be changes in the leadership of the opposition parties. In the USA the year will end with revelations of criminal involvement in the financial system. In Italy there will be a new government, one which favours the splitting of the country into northern and southern halves. It is very likely that NATO troops will be in action, though in a peacekeeping role, and it is unlikely that shots will be fired. A change of government in Bangladesh, with much popular protest, will provide a temporary solution to the year's upheavals. Businesses can expect a boom Christmas.

The King George IV Chase at Kempton may be won by the second favourite.

Please name FOULSHAM'S ALMANACK when replying to Advertisers

MANDRAKE PRESS — NEW AGE, OCCULT & METAPHYSICAL BOOKS

A Small Selection from our Catalogues

❏ Spiritual Healing	£5.99	❏ Spellcraft, Hexcraft & Witchcraft	£4.50
❏ Love Spells	£4.99	❏ Candle Burning Magic	£4.95
❏ Clairvoyance	£7.50	❏ Golden Secrets of Mystic Oils	£4.95
❏ The Sixth Sense	£6.50	❏ Magic with Incense & Powders	£4.95
❏ Christian Healing	£7.95	❏ Powers of the Psalms	£4.95
❏ Myths & Dreams	£11.95	❏ Black & White Magic	£2.95
❏ Practical Psychometry	£6.50	❏ Magic Circle	£4.50
❏ Gypsy Sorcery	£18.00	❏ Spiritual Workers Handbook	£4.50
❏ Philosophy of Witchcraft	£9.95	❏ Witch's Spellcraft	£4.50
❏ Crystal Magic	£3.50	❏ Witch's Broomstick Manual	£4.50
❏ Magick for Lovers	£3.50	❏ Wizards Bible	£4.50
❏ Have You Been Cursed	£3.50	❏ Truth About Astral Projection	£1.99
❏ Read the Tarot in Seven Days	£3.50	❏ Truth About Crystal Healing	£1.99
❏ Rune Magick	£3.50	❏ Truth About Hypnosis	£1.99
❏ Making Magical Tools & Equipment	£3.50	❏ Truth About Psychic Powers	£1.99
❏ So You Want to be a Witch	£3.50	❏ Truth About Psychic Self-defence	£1.99
❏ How to use a Ouija Board	£3.50	❏ Truth About The Druids	£1.99
❏ Easy Astral Projection	£3.50	❏ Truth About Past Life Regression	£1.99
❏ Simple Candle Magic	£3.50	❏ Truth About Runes	£1.99
❏ Prayer Book	£4.95	❏ Truth About Shamanism	£1.99
❏ Secrets of Magical Seals	£4.50	❏ Truth About Egyptian Magick	£1.99

★ *FREE* THE BLUE BOOK
88 page Catalogue of 1400 titles from the World's leading New Age and Occult Publishers. All orders are processed and despatched from stock within 24 hours of receipt.

★ *FREE* THE YELLOW BOOK
The biggest mail order list in the World? A Catalogue of Metaphysical books - the Mandrake Press 96 Page Special Order Catalogue. Choose from over 12,000 USA titles.

★ **FREE CATALOGUES** *

★ **FREE POST & PACKING ON ALL ORDERS**

★ **PRICES UP TO 40% BELOW OTHER MAIL ORDER SUPPLIERS**

*Overseas Customers please send £2.00 sterling

MANDRAKE PRESS LTD. FREEPOST, THAME, OX9 3BR
No Stamp Required

❏ PLEASE RUSH ME YOUR FREE CATALOGUES

NAME ....

ADDRESS ....

....

....

POST CODE ....

TELEPHONE 0844 217567

. .47. .

Cont'd from p. 33

LEO BORN PEOPLE

SEPTEMBER INFLUENCES: 1-2nd Exercise as much control over the circumstances of your own life as you are able to do. 14-15th Work seems to be on your mind, even if you are fettered by matters of a more domestic nature. 29-30th Advantages that come along now are unexpected and need to be dealt with carefully. OPPORTUNITIES: 12-13th Look out for people who are in a position to do you a great deal of personal good. LIMITING INFLUENCES: 25-26th Don't try to manipulate.

OCTOBER INFLUENCES: 3-4th The people you know the best can be of tremendous use to you now, both materially and personally. 16-17th The harder you work at this time, the better the long-term prospects. 29-30th Plenty of support is on hand, some of it from surprising directions. OPPORTUNITIES: 9-10th Any celebrations that come along now arrive via friends and their special support. LIMITING INFLUENCES: 24-25th Your real worth barely shines out.

NOVEMBER INFLUENCES: 2-3rd Personally speaking you are on top form, though family members are very demanding. 10-11th People who have problems are now inclined to turn to you for support. 24-25th The brakes are put upon personal efforts, if only for a day or two. OPPORTUNITIES: 5-6th Apparent disadvantages can now be turned in your direction. LIMITING INFLUENCES: 19-20th Not everyone you come across seems to care about you all that much.

DECEMBER INFLUENCES: 1-2nd Almost from the start of the month you have your plans in mind for the weeks ahead. 13-14th What you want and what you actually can achieve are two different things. 29-30th You find some warm and interesting people to help share your leisure time. OPPORTUNITIES: 25-26th An excellent Christmas period, with time and energy to get out and about. LIMITING INFLUENCES: 16-17th Things generally do not have the pace and speed that you would really wish.

VIRGO BORN PEOPLE

Birthdays between August 24th and September 23rd inclusive. Your planet is Mercury. Birthstone, sardonyx. Lucky day, Wednesday.

KEYNOTE FOR THE YEAR Confidence to do the things that you know are right is on the increase with 1995, though you may find that things generally take a little while to get going.

JANUARY INFLUENCES: 1-2nd Standard responses don't work very well at the start of the year, so try to be original. 12-13th It isn't easy to conform to expected patterns, though you can if you really try. 27-28th Creative potential is good and you want to try your hand at all manner of new skills. OPPORTUNITIES: 15-16th Plan an adventure, this is just the time to do so. LIMITING INFLUENCES: 25-26th Acting on impulse could be a mistake.

FEBRUARY INFLUENCES: 1-2nd Try to lay out detailed plans for the month. 19-20th A large push towards longed-for objectives is indicated. 27-28th You are shrewd, calculating and able. OPPORTUNITIES: 15-16th The support coming in from outside can prove to be of tremendous help at this stage, so don't turn it away. LIMITING INFLUENCES: 21-22nd Routines are very hard to come to terms with.

MARCH INFLUENCES: 2-3rd Don't turn away from a genuine cry for help that comes your way now. 14-15th Friends can be especially sweet at this time and try to help you out. 22-23rd Because you are so reasonable, others try to be so too. OPPORTUNITIES: 20-21st A better time with regard to your finances. LIMITING INFLUENCES: 12-13th You may expect far more from life than you find it is able to offer.

VIRGO BORN PEOPLE

APRIL INFLUENCES: 3-4th Be bold and adventurous, and don't allow your intentions to be thwarted. 17-18th Anxiety is minimised as you create a more relaxed atmosphere, both for yourself and those around you. 24-25th Keeping yourself committed to the task in hand may not be easy. OPPORTUNITIES: 12-13th Good luck comes your way, perhaps from an unexpected direction. LIMITING INFLUENCES: 28-29th Not everything that you have in mind is going to turn out entirely as you might have hoped.

MAY INFLUENCES: 1-2nd A good start to the month, though slower than you might have hoped. 14-15th Give and take are important, and probably in equal proportion during this time. 22-23rd There are few obstacles in your path, and those that you do notice should only be minor ones. OPPORTUNITIES: 17-19th Genuine affection surrounds you, even if you may fail to notice its presence at first. LIMITING INFLUENCES: 26-27th It's possible that you do not feel particularly brave and need to look for support.

JUNE INFLUENCES: 3-4th Use your communication skills to gain your objectives. 14-15th A useful interval, though more so in a social sense than financially speaking. 22-23rd Preparing for celebrations of some sort might take up a fair percentage of your time. OPPORTUNITIES: 29th New people coming into your life have an important part to play. LIMITING INFLUENCES: 26-27th Useful contacts can be lost unless you are paying attention.

JULY INFLUENCES: 1-2nd You are about to get a sneak preview at new practical potentials. 14-15th Acting out a role that is expected of you can prove to be time-consuming and problematical. 26-27th Rest and relaxation are the best keys to success, at least for the moment. OPPORTUNITIES: 25th Things hot up generally, and money matters are less difficult for you to deal with. LIMITING INFLUENCES: 19-21st Turning your mind to practical matters is not at all easy and your level of concentration is slipping.

AUGUST INFLUENCES: 1-3rd A slow start to the month, but quite positive all the same. 12-13th All incentives come from outside of your own life. 22-23rd Genuine wisdom is hard to come by, though intuition is as strong as you could wish. 29th An unusual attitude has to be dealt with. OPPORTUNITIES: 15-17th Friends are especially reasonable, and can be a great help to you. LIMITING INFLUENCES: 18-19th Incentive is hard to find, and the help of friends could just help to redress the balance.

SEPTEMBER INFLUENCES: 2-3rd You have time on your side when it comes to planning of almost any sort. 14-15th Romance is in the air and most Virgoans will want to make the most of it. 22-24th Standard responses are really of little use. What you need now is genuine originality. 29th A friend has a particularly good idea. OPPORTUNITIES: 17-18th It is particularly easy to smile at this time, and to turn smiles into advantages. LIMITING INFLUENCES: 25-26th Space to be yourself is limited.

OCTOBER INFLUENCES: 2-3rd Utilise any skill you possess to gain your objectives in life. 5-6th A realisation of your true worth is useful during these two days. 16-17th Creative potential is extremely strong and can be turned to your advantage. 26-27th The stranger the situation, the better you are able to deal with it now. OPPORTUNITIES: 18-19th A very good time to take risks, especially in a financial sense. LIMITING INFLUENCES: 29-30th Acting a part in life will not really help you at all.

NOVEMBER INFLUENCES: 4-5th A review of your financial potential is required close to the start of the month. 13-14th Relatives and friends alike have an important part to play in your decision making. 21-22nd Avoid clinging to others more than you have to. OPPORTUNITIES: 9-10th There is time for almost anything now, though perhaps you should take life a little more slowly. LIMITING INFLUENCES: 15-16th It could seem that people are against you, though the fault is your own.

DECEMBER INFLUENCES: 1-2nd Right from the start of the month, you have your mind set on Christmas. 5-6th Confidence is high, don't waste the possibilities of it. 19-20th Convention is for the birds, opt for originality if you can. OPPORTUNITIES: 25-26th A very interesting and entertaining Christmas period is in store for you. LIMITING INFLUENCES: 29-30th There could be some doubts about as the year draws to its end, though these are not too important and should not be allowed to hold you back.

Rub – Rub – Rub – "it works"

THE GOLDEN RABBIT'S FOOT FOR LUCK

Do you need lots of cash. Are you head-over-heels in debt? Would it take a lot of luck to solve **all** your problems.

Then, here my Friend, is the news you've been waiting and praying for.

Now for the very first time, you can possess the all-powerful symbol of the age-old, time-tested lucky charm . . . THE GOLDEN RABBIT'S FOOT!

Applauded by men and women all over the world for the mysterious way it attracts good luck! Just by rubbing its gleaming, golden paw!

I invite you to join me in a test to see if this age old mystic legend is really true.

But the best is yet to come! To make this offer so irresistible that you'll send the coupon below RIGHT AWAY I'm going to make you a promise.

You MUST agree that the mystic legend is absolutely 100% true — and that the GOLDEN RABBIT'S FOOT actually does bring you the luck you've always wanted by just "rubbing" its foot — or I'll refund your money GUARANTEED ONE-HUNDRED PER CENT!

But before we go further, let me assure you of this crystal-clear fact: I know EXACTLY what I'm doing. I wouldn't dare make such an offer if I thought for one moment that I would lose! So for your own sake, simply send £12 today to receive your very own GOLDEN RABBIT'S FOOT.

Do you want lots of luck and money NOW, immediately, and continuing for as long as you rub the GOLDEN RABBIT'S FOOT? Do you want this sensational opportunity to wipe out your bad luck and financial problems?

Imagine the excitement and thrill of turning your situation AROUND just be rubbing your bad luck away.

. . . When you want to pay off debts, simply rub the lucky GOLDEN RABBIT'S FOOT!

. . . When you want to buy a new car, simply rub the lucky GOLDEN RABBIT'S FOOT!

. . . When you want to buy a fantastic holiday, simply rub the lucky GOLDEN RABBIT'S FOOT!

. . . When you want to have ALL OF LIFE'S REWARDS, simply rub the lucky GOLDEN RABBIT'S FOOT!

TELL ME EVERY TIME THE GOLDEN RABBIT'S FOOT BRINGS MONEY MIRACLES

Whenever your GOLDEN RABBIT'S FOOT puts all the money you want in your pocket . . . whenever you enjoy the fabulous thrill of getting rid of tormenting overdue bills . . . whenever you WIN £100, £1,000, even £10,000 or MORE playing the horses, cards, bingo, the lottery, any games of chance, just let me know everything — just as it happened!

Even if you are a non-believer you have absolutely nothing in the world to lose. Not one single penny of your hard-earned money. Because from the moment you receive the GOLDEN RABBIT'S FOOT, you must receive fantastic INSTANT Good Luck, or I'll return your money GUARANTEED!

That's right! It doesn't matter who you are, where you live, what kind of INSTANT GOOD LUCK you need! You MUST AGREE that the GOLDEN RABBIT'S FOOT can make any wish come true immediately, or I'll return your money.

SEND FOR YOUR GOLDEN RABBIT'S FOOT AT ONCE WITHOUT RISK!

Right now, this very minute, I want you to send the coupon for your own GOLDEN RABBIT'S FOOT. Right away.

Your GOLDEN RABBIT'S FOOT will be rushed back to you in YOUR NAME ONLY. No one else will be allowed to use its amazing miracles, except you. Just follow the simple directions included FREE — and see for yourself.

100% MONEY BACK GUARANTEE

I cannot imagine anyone no matter how sceptical they may be, passing up this unique opportunity to join this Research Project and use the legendary GOLDEN RABBIT'S FOOT every single day. If the only thing holding you back is taking a risk, I will eliminate that doubt completely, because I honestly believe that the GOLDEN RABBIT'S FOOT can work miracles for you.

I'll give you this fantastic 100% money-back guarantee. GOLDEN RABBIT'S FOOT must work for YOU within a mere 30 days, or I'll return ALL your money. Just send me the coupon below and £10 NOW. It may be the answer to ALL your money problems.

Print your name and address on the coupon. Include your £12 cheque, postal order or cash, and send to:

Marie Simone, Dept OM95R TOTTERIDGE VILLAGE LONDON N20 8PN

GOLDEN RABBIT'S FOOT COUPON

Marie Simone, Dept OM94R
TOTTERIDGE VILLAGE
LONDON N20 8PN

RUB THE GOLDEN RABBIT'S FOOT

I enclose £12.00 herewith, please send me my GOLDEN RABBIT'S FOOT in a private unmarked package. Money-back in 30 days if not absolutely thrilled with results.

Name ....

Address ....

.... Date of Birth ....

☐ Rush me TWO orders! Here's £22 for both. Same guarantee!

YES! A GUARANTEED DOUBLE PROMISE!

The unique design of this GOLDEN RABBIT'S FOOT harnesses good luck powers. Powers so potent and so astounding, that results are ABSOLUTELY GUARANTEED, with a full money-back refund.

When you receive the GOLDEN RABBIT'S FOOT, expect to experience amazing results of MONEY, LOVE, AND HEALTH — *like nothing else you've seen before*, backed by this guaranteed 100% PROMISE of a full money-back refund.

If not thrilled, return it within 30 days. Your money will be refunded IN FULL.

LIBRA BORN PEOPLE

**Birthdays between September 24th and October 23rd inclusive.
Your planet is Venus. Birthstone, opal. Lucky day, Friday.**

KEYNOTE FOR THE YEAR   Give and take are important factors at any stage this year, though since both come as second nature to your sign, you should achieve more in a general sense than even you might expect.

JANUARY INFLUENCES: 1-2nd A steady start to the year but some personal irritations are inclined to be restricting. 11-12th At this time you are likely to discover help coming from the least expected directions. 20th Better progress in all practical matters, though not a time for thinking too much. 25th Very much in the limelight socially speaking, whilst other people are enjoying their own successes. OPPORTUNITIES: 27-28th It becomes much easier to sort out difficulties and cut through red tape at this time. LIMITING INFLUENCES: 13-14th Much longed for projects are shelved, leading to annoyance.

FEBRUARY INFLUENCES: 1-2nd An excellent start to new projects, with work aspects especially favourable. 8-10th Good news arrives from a variety of different sources and finances strengthen. 18-19th Domestic issues need some discussion and a flexible attitude. 21st A developing need arises to cut losses professionally and re-think plans. OPPORTUNITIES: 24-25th Gains through administrative bodies or authority figures. LIMITING INFLUENCES: 15-16th You may be too much inclined to dwell on past difficulties instead of future projects.

MARCH INFLUENCES: 2-3rd Good progress in a workaday sense and with regard to new friendships. 10-11th Friends put you under unfair pressure, though not if you act sensibly. 20-21st People are very kind, and happy to be as much help as they can be. 26-27th All in all this should be perhaps the most promising period of the month, personally as well as financially. OPPORTUNITIES: 5-6th Good luck and better prosperity are in store for the Libran subject. LIMITING INFLUENCES: 18-19th Unexpected happenings cause many delays and create the odd argument.

APRIL INFLUENCES: 1-2nd There are difficult details to be dealt with as the month commences, though colleagues should be helpful. 10-11th Some indecision is possible, followed by an over dynamic quality that could spell trouble. 18-19th Back your own instincts and don't be swayed by wayward opinions. 29-30th Put some distance between yourself and the negative attitudes of friends. OPPORTUNITIES: 7-8th Profitable contacts, especially in a financial sense. LIMITING INFLUENCES: 21-22nd Some dissatisfaction with life can slow down otherwise good progress.

MAY INFLUENCES: 2-3rd An ideal time for getting yourself the finer things in life to a greater degree than recently. 6-7th An increase in pressure, both from work and regarding the needs of friends. 14-15th Some restlessness arrives,but also the ability to make financial progress. 22-23rd This is a period when your natural diplomacy really begins to show itself. OPPORTUNITIES: 12-13th A new phase of action and intense activity. LIMITING INFLUENCES: 24-26th Turning away from social possibilities at this stage is not to be recommended.

JUNE INFLUENCES: 1-2nd Not a promising start to the month, with some lack of opportunity. 13-14th Despite positive expectations some delays seem likely. 20-21st You may find yourself becoming aware that not everything is quite as it seems. 24-25th It is all too easy to fall out with friends, some of whom are behaving strangely. 28-29th A time of alterations and new assessments in a workaday sense. OPPORTUNITIES: 15-16th You have confidence and energy to spare. LIMITING INFLUENCES: 30th Some of the actions of people you care about are now quite mystifying.

JULY INFLUENCES: 2-3rd The best chance this week for making up your mind about future possibilities. 7-8th One-to-one relationships are now finding a new footing and offering rewards. 15-16th You might feel that you are not making quite the progress that you would wish, though don't allow this to prevent you from trying. 26-27th Small gestures on the part of other people can bring out the best in your own efforts. OPPORTUNITIES: 18-19th An especially high point in personal terms and in your appreciation of others. LIMITING INFLUENCES: 4-5th Routines hold you back for a day or two.

Please name FOULSHAM'S ALMANACK when replying to Advertisers

OURS IS ...

PROBABLY THE MOST UNUSUAL CATALOGUE IN THE WORLD!

Our information tapes, books and publications can help you to achieve life goals, self improvement and therapeutic benefits. 4 × 1st class stamps brings 400 item descriptive brochure of our whole range:

CASSETTES	£	CASSETTES	£
How to Learn Anything Whilst Sleeping	8.95	Don't Work Hard – Work Smart	8.95
The Case for Early Learning in Children	8.95	The Science of Getting Rich	8.95
How to Create a Super Intelligent Child	8.95	Overcoming Sleeping Problems	8.95
Exceptionally Fast Learning Techniques	8.95	Hair Today – Hair Tomorrow	8.95
Writing Your Own Life Script	8.95	Stopping or Controlling Drinking	8.95
How to Survive a Recession	8.95	Super Memory Improvement Techniques	8.95
After the Divorce – The Years Ahead	8.95	Increasing Your Energy	8.95
Anyone Can Write – Even You	8.95	Ending Loneliness	8.95
Overcoming Fear of Flying	8.95	How to Stop Being Embarrassed	8.95
Getting Rid of Cellulite	8.95	The Art of Commencing and Maintaining Conversation	8.95
How to Get a Job	8.95	50 Ways to Reduce Everyday Stress	8.95
How to Chat Up Any Female – Anywhere	8.95	Bible Quotations Interpreted III	8.95
The 10 Best Ways to Attract Females	8.95	The Power of Prayer	8.95
How to Make Love to Almost Any Woman You Meet	8.95	The Reason and Purpose of Human Life	8.95
How to Make Love – Better	8.95	How Human Beings Can Live Eternally	8.95
Enhancing Your Sex Life	8.95	Spiritual Healing Technique	8.95
Sex for the Over Sixties	8.95	The Four Horsemen of the Apocalypse Fully Explained	8.95
Overcoming Prem. Ejaculation	8.95	A Method of Psychic Healing	4.95
Being Your Own Sex Therapist	8.95	How to Cast Spells	8.95
How to be Adored by Men	8.95	Developing E.S.P.	8.95
Super Nutrition for Super Sport Performance	8.95	Practical Time Travel Techniques	8.95
Psyching Yourself Up for Peak Sport Performance	8.95	Occult Secrets Revealed	8.95
Making Money Through Classified Ads	8.95	World Prophecy 1990-2040	8.95

New Era Tapes & Publications (OM5), 15 Royal Crescent, Cheltenham, Glos GL50 3DA

Almanack Readers Offer:

Start collecting the worlds most powerful charms right now
and you will receive a wonderful FREE 'I CHING' READING with this order.

☐ ✔ JAPANESE INSTANT MONEY CHARM

Some of the worlds richest and most successful people bless the day they owned this fabulous wealth creating talisman. Career success, wins of money, cars, houses. Never be poor again. USE FOR LOTTERIES, POOLS, RACING, BINGO, SPOT THE BALL. Jim. 'Is it magic or belief that makes it work? last month I won £282,000.'

☐ ✔ CHINESE HEALTH CHARM

The Western world often chooses to treat anxiety and stress with drugs. But now the worlds oldest civilization is beginning to share its secrets. A thousand years of folklore have gone into making this amazing herbal charm. Mind over matter. To dispel anxiety, and instill a powerful inner confidence.

☐ ✔ TIBETAN LOVE CHARM

To attract new love or rekindle an old flame. To bring family and friends together. End quarrels. Bring harmony, joy, and happiness.

Guaranteed to work or **will refund.** Yes, all charms must work! These unique items are valuable collectors pieces. However ... you can put them to the test entirely at my risk. If fantastic good fortune and the best good luck in the world does not begin to bless you, then simply return for a full refund. You will still get to keep and enjoy your super *FREE 'I CHING' READING*.
I accept all the risk ... there is no risk to you at all ... **you can only get lucky.**
So start collecting now and you could be enjoying 'ALL THE LUCK IN THE WORLD'
As a special to ALMANACK readers these beautiful Charms are amazingly only £5 each or £15 for all 3 charms.
Cash/cheque/p.o. .... or o.k. to pay by Visa/Access. Card no. .... Expire date ....

Name .... Address ....

.... Post Code ....

EDWARD KIND, PO BOX 29, SWADLINCOTE, DERBYSHIRE, DE11 0GG

. .52. .

LIBRA BORN PEOPLE

AUGUST   INFLUENCES: 1-2nd Affairs of the heart bring both positive and negative possibilities. 11-12th Softer and more sensitive now, you have a need to show love for others. 15-16th This is a very challenging interlude but has definite high spots. 20-21st An increase of professional confidence and better decision making. 28th Be certain that your motivations are right. OPPORTUNITIES: 22-23rd The best days for general opportunities and for long-term planning. LIMITING INFLUENCES: 7th A realisation of past mistakes can lead to negative attitudes.

SEPTEMBER   INFLUENCES: 1-2nd Social and business gatherings are very important and bring rewards. 5-7th Brings a need for relaxation from personal pressures and difficult relationships. 15-16th Look out for news from far away that could lead to better prospects later. 20-21st Gains come to the private sphere of your life and via personal relationships. 28-29th Unexpected contacts bring good news and new possibilities. OPPORTUNITIES: 25-26th A busy spell but beneficial in unusual ways. LIMITING INFLUENCES: 10-11th Possible low spirits leading to general lethargy.

OCTOBER   INFLUENCES: 1-2nd An excellent beginning to the month with plenty of enthusiasm. 5-6th A cheerful optimism and some favourable contacts. 18-19th look out for a very romantic period with plenty of personal attention. 21-22nd Social prospects especially good as people warm in attitude. 26th Less favourable personally, possibly because you lack an understanding of people's needs. OPPORTUNITIES: 28-29th Luck is especially good, personally and financially. LIMITING INFLUENCES: 13-14th A slowing down of trends generally and some bad luck.

NOVEMBER   INFLUENCES: 1-2nd You are very light hearted and able to turn even difficult situations to your advantage. 6-7th Don't rely too much on promises from other people, but act on your own hunches. 16-17th Too many mood swings. Slow life down and control it instead of it ruling you. 21-22nd A renewed need for travel and great change in your social life. 27-28th Make the most of the goodwill that others are showing now. OPPORTUNITIES: 3-4th You are able to take charge of the circumstances of your own life. LIMITING INFLUENCES: 14-15th A general lull, with difficulty making progress.

DECEMBER   INFLUENCES: 1-2nd A good start to the month, especially regarding social trends. 7-8th An ambitious interlude and especially good for alterations to working schedules. 21st Restless and needing change, don't react aggresively. 27-28th Too occupied with domestic issues and in need of security. 31st You have a positive attitude to the New Year. OPPORTUNITIES: 5-6th Optimism and energy are especially high. LIMITING INFLUENCES: 18th Hasty actions are definitely out at this stage.

 # SCORPIO BORN PEOPLE

Birthdays between October 24th and November 22nd inclusive. Your planets are Mars and Pluto. Birthstone, topaz. Lucky day, Tuesday.

KEYNOTE FOR THE YEAR   It is only a matter of time before you find that you are getting yourself into a more comfortable position generally, though things may be quieter at the start of 1995.

JANUARY   INFLUENCES: 1-2nd You have good prospects in store, as long as you recognise them now. 19-20th A big push towards favoured objectives in a practical sense. 30-31st It is important to stay as optimistic as possible, particularly with regard to work. OPPORTUNITIES: 15-16th You look towards social possibilities with a great deal of enthusiasm and some success. LIMITING INFLUENCES: 6-7th The penalty for trying to do too much is becoming more tired than is really good for you.

Please name FOULSHAM'S ALMANACK when replying to Advertisers

Why be a star-crossed lover?

Explore the hidden truths of astral compatibility. And see how faithfully the secrets of the Zodiac mirror the secrets of the heart.

True loving partnerships are made in heaven - as confirmed by endless comparisons of birth charts, with their tell-tale signals and portents for mutual happiness.

Now study this important new guide to love and the Zodiac by a top professional astrologer, based on her first-hand knowledge of thousands of individual case histories. You'll quickly acquire valuable insights into the astral link between any two people on earth. And gain a major advantage in your planning of relationships.

You may want to keep this knowledge to yourself as a secret trump card in your pursuit of love. Or you may prefer to share it with others and become a trusted expert in this coveted branch of astral wisdom, relevant to so many but revealed to so few.

This is much, much more than just a Yes/No checklist of birth signs. It's an in-depth analysis of each cross-zodiac relationship, charting the separate implications for the male and the female of each sign, including couples both born under the same one.

What exactly is it that makes Taurus women love Cancer men? Why do Scorpio and Aquarius just never get on? And who is best placed to melt the shy Miss Virgo?

You'll get a total overview of these partnerships, from the meeting of physical passions to the interplay of different talents and intellects, and the prospect of lasting, loving friendships. For a deeper understanding of those hidden influences that direct our lives behind the scenes.

Unashamedly frank revelations.

In this detailed emotional portrait, the author does not fob you off with vague terms or tactful euphemisms. You want the blunt truth. And it is here - with startlingly plain references to the roots of sexual compatibility.

Now start investigating the fascinating and well proven links between astral harmony and personal rapport. And see how the signs of the Zodiac can be used as reliable signposts to happiness and fulfilment.

For your copy of **Love, Sex & Astrology**, send cheque/PO for just **£5.50** to Globe Book Services, Brunel Rd., Houndmills, Basingstoke, Hants, RG21 2XS. Price includes p&p. Allow 28 days for delivery.

FACULTY OF ASTROLOGICAL STUDIES

FOUNDED 1948

The Finest and Most Comprehensive Astrological Tuition in the World

The Faculty teaches astrology by correspondence courses, evening classes, seminars and summer schools. Training includes the Certificate Course which takes students from beginners to intermediate level, the intermediate course, and the Diploma course which is a fully comprehensive and up-to-date professional training programme of three years duration, leading to the Faculty's internationally recognised Diploma (D.F.Astrol.S.).

Consultants lists available.

Details: Ref. OMA, Registrar, FAS 396 Caledonian Road, London N1 1DN.
Tel: 071-700 3556 (24 hr answering) Fax: 071-700 6479.

Counselling Within Astrology Course. Open to suitable applicants. **Details: Registrar, Tel: 0494 676675**

HAIR LOSS

The safe, easy, inexpensive Herbal Treatment for men and women.

BUY THREE AND GET ONE FREE

For **FREE** literature send SAE to:
A. MOORE, M.I.P.I.
19 Abbotts Walk, Fleetwood, Lancs FY7 6QF
Please allow 28 days for delivery

JOHN DORAN
Internationally Known Healer
7th Son of a 7th Son

Offers healing in the most simple and oldest method to those that cannot get help from other sources of treatments. Animals also treated.
Absent healing a speciality.
Write to: **John Doran, Avalon, Barton Street, Tinahely, Co. Wicklow, Eire**
Phone 010-353-402-38326

SCORPIO BORN PEOPLE

FEBRUARY INFLUENCES: 1-2nd There are some good ideas about, so be prepared to use them. 15-16th Arguments at home should be seen as a storm in a teacup and not overplayed. 27-28th A good period financially, though some care is necessary in a personal sense. OPPORTUNITIES: 12-13th So much give and take as you show now is certain to prove useful in the end. LIMITING INFLUENCES: 23-24th A difficult atmosphere generally is very hard to counter. Tact is necessary.

MARCH INFLUENCES: 3-4th Most people are willing to put themselves out on your behalf, though you may have to ask. 12-13th Extra responsibilities can weigh heavily on your mind for a day or two. 21-22nd Imagination is not lacking, though practical skills could be for a short while. 30th Give and take help you to feather your own nest. OPPORTUNITIES: 15-16th Using your intuition is a good thing right now. LIMITING INFLUENCES: 24-25th Unreasonable people seem to cross your path in all spheres of life now.

APRIL INFLUENCES: 1-2nd Get tedious jobs out of the way as soon as you are able. 7-8th The intervention of a friend comes just at the right time to be of assistance. 27th Be brave when involved in social encounters. 30th A good and positive end to the month, though money could be tight. OPPORTUNITIES: 9-10th You have a great ability to get what you want from others. LIMITING INFLUENCES: 16-17th Creating the right social impression is far from easy at present.

MAY INFLUENCES: 2-3rd You take note of the season and tend to respond positively in kind. 12-13th Tedious jobs tend to take great self-discipline and some sacrifice. 22-23rd A time when you may be missing someone you love very much. OPPORTUNITIES: 19-20th This time tends to be a riot of colour and activity, with some good luck. LIMITING INFLUENCES: 30-31st A poor time, mainly because of your own attitudes, which are not all they could be for a short while.

JUNE INFLUENCES: 1-2nd Stay out there in the flow of life and don't be distracted from practical necessities. 13-14th Still inclined to follow the line of least resistance and not too positive generally. 24-25th All sorts of people tend to be of use to you for these two days. Make the most of the situation. OPPORTUNITIES: 16-17th With more money about, you are anxious to plan carefully and probably to spend wisely. LIMITING INFLUENCES: 21-22nd Paper transactions should all be checked carefully.

JULY INFLUENCES 2-3rd Don't try to move any mountains so early in the month. Some care is necessary. 14-15th Not everyone appears to have your best interests at heart, though they probably do in reality. 24-25th A stand-alone period, when you tend to stick up for yourself very well indeed. OPPORTUNITIES: 27-28th Conforming is easy and you make the most favourable impression on those in authority. LIMITING INFLUENCES: 21-22nd It isn't easy to be bright and cheerful, especially with others being so unhelpful.

AUGUST INFLUENCES: 1-2nd Situations beyond your own control seem to hold you back, if only for a very short while. 10-11th A suitable time for change of house or alterations to your present abode. 24-25th Standard responses are not much use, try to be as original as you can be. OPPORTUNITIES: 15-16th With good company and a social interlude in store, make the most of this period. LIMITING INFLUENCES: 30-31st Almost everyone seems to countermand your instructions or stand in your way.

SEPTEMBER INFLUENCES: 2-4th Not everything you do has the desired results at first but may do so eventually. 21-22nd Rewards do not necessarily come from expected directions. 24-25th Confidence is hardly high, but intuition should be strong enough. 30th Extend yourself in known tasks. OPPORTUNITIES: 12-13th A luckier period and one that brings unexpected gains. LIMITING INFLUENCES: 1516th Less energy, and a need to take significant amounts of rest during the day and evening alike.

OCTOBER INFLUENCES: 2-3rd All your imagination is necessary if you want to lift this period. 13-14th Complications, if they do arise now, tend to come from the direction of your family. 20-21st Confidence is on the increase, though not in terms of professional matters. OPPORTUNITIES: 24-25th Snap decisions could be the best ones to assure instant successes materially. LIMITING INFLUENCES: 22-23rd An active time, though not as fortunate as you might have wished or anticipated.

Please name FOULSHAM'S ALMANACK when replying to Advertisers

The healing arts of Aromatherapy

A jasmine bath for relieving tension and relaxing muscles... the soothing sweetness of a lavender and almond massage... the refreshing air of cedar or sandalwood burned like incense around the home...

Nature's own essences are known to work wonders for our health and mental well-being in the best traditions of drug-free holistic medicine.

Now read this practical guide

"...recognised by health and beauty writers as one of the best introductions to aromatherapy"
CHAT Magazine

to the ingredients, the techniques and the proven benefits of aromatherapy in treating a whole range of conditions from asthma and rheumatism to migraine or sunburn. See how these essential oils can be absorbed safely into the system, with profound and lasting effects on physical and spiritual harmony. And enjoy for yourself the bracing tang of an aromatic shower or the restful balm of reflexology with herbal lotions. It could make a big difference to all the family's health and happiness.

The Complete Book of Family Aromatherapy £7.50

... and the psychic energies that can be liberated by these scented oils

The deep significance of aromatics in natural magic. How various scents awaken psychic awareness and focus unseen earth-energies on our mind and spirit, vividly heightening direct visualisation. The fascinating mythology of herbs with their planetary and elemental links. By Scott Cunningham, a major New Age author on herbal magic and incense rituals.

Magical Aromatherapy.......£4.50

Send cheque/PO to Globe Book Services, Brunel Rd., Houndmills, Basingstoke, Hants, RG21 2XS. Price includes p&p. Allow 28 days for delivery.

"MANA MAGICK GETS RESULTS IN 3 DAYS"
Says DAVID SAVAGE, author of 'Mana Magick'

"It can sometimes take longer, but three days is normal. Mana Magick WORKS and it can obtain for you almost anything your heart desires!" It can bring you: WINS IN BINGO, POOLS AND LOTTERIES — A PAY INCREASE — THE MAN OR WOMAN YOU DESIRE — AN END TO ILLNESS AND DISEASE — INFLUENCE OVER IMPORTANT PEOPLE — A SOLUTION TO ANY FINANCIAL PROBLEM, NO MATTER HOW PRESSING — WIN BACK THE LOVE OF ANOTHER — GAIN THE RESPECT OF PEOPLE — BUILD SELF-CONFIDENCE — MAKE YOU CHARMING TO THE OPPOSITE SEX — BRING YOU GOOD LUCK EVERY DAY ... and more!

MANA MAGICK is safe and simple, and can be safely used by any religious person without violation of his or her beliefs. It is absolutely safe and simple for anyone and everyone.

MANA MAGICK has been used by mystics for centuries for solving their personal problems: IT CAN MYSTICALLY SOLVE ANY PROBLEM NOW FACING YOU. It can get you the job or position you now seek, it can end loneliness and open your life to friends and admirers, it can bring harmony at home and work, it can help you to see into the future, it can strengthen your concentration and memory. And it can begin getting results for you in just 3 days in most cases!

David Savage has been teaching MANA MAGICK to people for several years. He is convinced that it holds the hidden key to unlocking the doors of opportunity, love, wealth and power! His students are reporting amazing good fortune which they are sure only

MANA MAGICK has brought. MANA MAGICK can not only improve your fortunes but can also change your feelings about yourself: it can END COMPLETELY feelings of shyness and inferiority ... it can INJECT YOUR PERSONALITY with a radiant, dynamic magnetism. It can make people want you and love you.

MANA MAGICK is like a kind of "Genie's Lamp" of the mind — it can literally MATERIALIZE almost any desire or wish you want fulfilled! It can change your life from failure to success, it can suddenly start bringing you money from unexpected sources, it can give you a strange hold over people, and it can also make you absolutely safe from the evil thoughts and intentions of unkind people.

MANA MAGICK puts at your beck and call the powers of the Cosmos, the untapped powers of your mind and the help of angels and spirit guides.

With MANA MAGICK you have the invisible world on your side! It can protect you from harm, injury and accidents!

David Savage, the author, can also be your friend and guide once you have bought his MANA MAGICK book. Write to him care of us and he will answer you! He is so certain that MANA MAGICK can do for you what other books cannot that he wants you to share his good experiences with him! (Of course you don't have to write to David if you don't wish to.)

Your life can begin changing today by ordering this very special book. It costs only £5.00.

To order your copy all you have to do is write "MANA MAGICK" on a piece of paper with your name and address and send a Postal Order or Cheque (made payable to Finbarr) for £5.00 to:

FINBARR INTERNATIONAL Dept. O
16 Turketel Road, Folkestone, Kent CT20 2PA

Overseas send £6.75. Add 50p if catalogue also required. Callers at this address only: 113 Dover Rd, Folkestone.
(We have advertised in Old Moore's since 1975.)

SCORPIO BORN PEOPLE

NOVEMBER INFLUENCES: 1-2nd Not a bad start to the month, but restricting in a personal and romantic sense. 14-15th half way through the month you may begin to find yourself flagging. 21-22nd A static time, though a favourable period for thinking and planning. 29-30th Huge successes are not likely and you need to push hard to achieve almost anything at all. OPPORTUNITIES: 16th Better financial prospects come as a result of past planning and present efforts. LIMITING INFLUENCES: 17-18th If perfection inside yourself is what you are looking for now, think again.

DECEMBER INFLUENCES: 2-3rd Your plans for Christmas begin early in the month and continue unabated. 12-13th Some surprise invitations lift the day no end. 21-22nd Creative impulses are strong in advance of Christmas and are directed towards home and family. OPPORTUNITIES: 25th An especially good set of aspects for enjoying what Christmas has to offer. LIMITING INFLUENCES: 15-16th Try not to take on any more than you have to in a social sense, or you could suffer a little later.

SAGITTARIUS BORN PEOPLE

**Birthdays between November 23rd and December 21st inclusive.
Your planet is Jupiter. Birthstone, turquoise. Lucky day, Thursday.**

KEYNOTE FOR THE YEAR   With more in the way of excitement to set the period apart as being something very special, you have everything to look forward to in 1995. Not everything runs smoothly, but there are advantages, even in difficulties.

JANUARY INFLUENCES: 1-2nd Confidence is high for the start of the year and looks set to remain so. 12-13th Create the right impression for changes in and around your home. 27-28th Actions speak louder than words in social encounters. OPPORTUNITIES: 15-16th This would be an ideal time for taking on more responsibility or for changing your job. LIMITING INFLUENCES: 22-23rd Rules and regulations are inclined to get on your nerves and you may be a little more irritable than of late.

FEBRUARY INFLUENCES: 3-4th Attitudes around you are rather difficult to understand, though it is important to at least try. 17-18th Old ideas now have to be looked at again, in the light of changing values. 26-28th Confidence reaches a peak, though friends are not quite as supportive as you may have hoped. OPPORTUNITIES: 14-15th Money matters are best dealt with at this time, whilst cash is in greater supply. LIMITING INFLUENCES: 19th Not everyone is helpful when it comes to new schemes.

MARCH INFLUENCES: 1-2nd A real bonus can be expected socially as the month opens. 15-16th It may be necessary to look again at finances, which could fluctuate wildly at this time. 24-25th A bold gesture on your part is likely to gain extra support from friends and relatives alike. OPPORTUNITIES: 27-28th There is no lack of confidence right now, and plenty to do with it. LIMITING INFLUENCE: 18-19th Arguments both in and out of your home should be avoided if at all possible, in favour of sensible discussion.

APRIL INFLUENCES: 2-3rd A not so bold Sagittarian finds some difficulty coming to terms with practical changes. 9-10th Out and about more than ever, you enjoy the cut and thrust of the social scene. 24-25th The ideas you have at the moment are a little out of the ordinary, so explain yourself. OPPORTUNITIES: 18-19th Confidence is high and money matters are more settled than for some time. LIMITING INFLUENCES: 29-30th A less than inspiring end to the month, probably because you lack some confidence at present.

Amazing Candle Rituals for Money, Love, etc.

GUARANTEED TO WORK — OR YOUR MONEY BACK!

At last! You can now use the ancient art of Candle Burning to gain your heart's desires — WITHOUT THE PROBLEM OF HAVING TO BUY ANY SPECIAL HERBS, OILS OR INCENSES! All you need is ordinary candles from your supermarket to get *powerful results* from the rituals in this book! And so simple are these rituals that even a child can perform them! *80 proven rituals* are given, including:

● **To Receive Money & Good Fortune . . . To Win in Bingo, Races, etc. . . . Win Someone's Love . . . Get a Legal Decision in Your Favour . . . Break-up Someone's Love Affair . . . Deliverance from an Unjust Situation . . . Bring Peace in the Family . . . Find a New Home . . . End Loneliness . . . Heal Another Person . . . Save a Failing Marriage . . . Make a Barren Womb Fruitful . . . To Ensure a Safe Pregnancy . . . Improve Concentration . . . Pass Exams . . . Defeat Evil Landlord . . . Punish a Violent Person . . . Reconcile a Broken Friendship . . . To Ensure a Safe Air Flight . . . Protection Against Sudden Death . . .** *and scores more!*

Whatever your need you will find a ritual to hlep you! All rituals are absolutely safe — and yet *more*

powerful than the complicated candle rituals of other books! And you don't have to be a witch to perform them — even practising Christians, Muslims and Jews can use them. Many of the rituals are in fact Bible-inspired!

If you think Candle Burning is superstitious nonsense then think again. Put it to the test. Try it to win somone's love or to receive money. You will be pleasantly surprised. This book shows how Candle Burning can in fact be very *scientific*, and it reveals how to get the art to start *working for you immediately.*

Every ritual has been *tried and proven.* We have files of testimonials from delighted readers (photo-copies of actual letters available on request). Many years of research went into these rituals before they were published in this book. And remember we *GUARANTEE* results. You *MUST* get results or return the book within *45 days for a full refund.*

To order Candle Burning Rituals by the New Age Fellowship **send just £6.95** to Finbarr International (OC), 16 Turketel Rd, Folkestone, Kent CT20 2PA. Overseas send £9.50. Catalogue 50p. Callers at this address only: 113 Dover Rd, Folkestone. *We have advertised in Old Moore's since 1975.*

Almanack Readers Offer:

Start collecting the worlds most powerful charms right now and you will receive a wonderful FREE RUNES READING with this order.

☐ ✔ *WIZARDS MONEY WINNING CHARM*

This powerful Pagan Charm demonstrates the magical wisdom of the ancients. It was specially created to attract great wins and finds of money, gold, silver,and jewels, believers say that you can actually FEEL it working when used for Lotteries, Pools, Bingo, Racing, Spot the Ball, etc. Jim. *'Is it magic or belief that makes it work? last month I won £282,000.'*

☐ ✔ *RUNE LOVE POWER CHARM*

Golden Rune writing upon Black Marble makes this an enchantingly beautiful Talisman. It calls upon natures magic to attract new love or to rekindle an old flame.

☐ ✔ *STONEHENGE WISHING STONE*

The Ancients really had something here.They treasured this stone and believed it made wishes come true. Even today owners tell of amazing results when wishing for love, wealth, exam passes, and success.

Many say the STONE begins to tingle in the palm of the hand as a wish is made. Most effective if used . . . with a request for 3 wishes to be granted. Choose wisely.

Guaranteed to work or **will refund.** Yes, all charms must work! These unique items are valuable collectors pieces. However . . . you can put them to the test entirely at my risk. If fantastic good fortune and the best good luck in the world does not begin to bless you, then simply return for a full refund. You will still get to keep and enjoy your super *FREE RUNES READING.*

I accept all the risk . . . there is no risk to you at all . . . **you can only get lucky.**

So start collecting now and you could be enjoying 'ALL THE LUCK IN THE WORLD'

As a special to ALMANACK readers these beautiful Charms are amazingly only £5 each or £15 for all 3 charms.

Cash/cheque/p.o. . . . or o.k. to pay by Visa/Access. Card no. .... Expire date ....

Name .... Address ....

.... Post Code ....

EDWARD KIND, PO BOX 29, SWADLINCOTE, DERBYSHIRE, DE11 0GG

SAGITTARIUS BORN PEOPLE

MAY INFLUENCES: 1-2nd Your ideas tend to fluctuate at this time and some continuity should be sought. 15-16th No matter how lacking you may be in drive, there are things that simply have to be done, so pitch in and have a go. 27-28th All your effort in the direction of friendship seems to have been worthwhile and there are invitations flooding in at this time. OPPORTUNITIES: 18-19th The things that other people say give food for positive thought. LIMITING INFLUENCES: 22-24th Less energy means having to draw your horns in regarding certain plans.

JUNE INFLUENCES: 2-3rd The attitudes of your friends are difficult to understand, though you will have to try. 9-10th Confidence is not high, but there is encouragement if you look for it. 24-25th Contribute to efforts designed to improve matters in and around your home. OPPORTUNITIES: 28-29th Even routines have more going for them than usually seems to be the case. LIMITING INFLUENCES: 15-16th Not everyone you come across is equally trustworthy and some scepticism is called for when dealing with strangers.

JULY INFLUENCES: 1-2nd The month opens with some interesting professional possibilities, but you might have to look for them. 16-17th Less dynamism about at this time and as a result it could be difficult to get yourself into gear with new projects. 20-21st Concrete plans show signs of crumbling under the pressure of changing circumstances. OPPORTUNITIES: 26-27th Retreating from situations is something that you would not dream of doing during this period. LIMITING INFLUENCES: 12-13th The attitude of relatives is a little difficult to understand.

AUGUST INFLUENCES: 1-2nd In terms of character you have plenty going for you at present, so make the most of it. 13-14th Rules and regulations tend to get on your nerves at this time and real patience is called for when dealing with them. 24-25th You might not be on top form but you still have the ability to turn a few heads on occasions. OPPORTUNITIES: 15-16th Confidence is on the increase, especially when you are dealing with work. LIMITING INFLUENCES: 19-20th Annoying delays will just have to be dealt with patiently.

SEPTEMBER INFLUENCES: 4-5th Be adventurous when it comes to the chance to take an outing of some sort. 19-20th Routines turn out to be a chore, so do what you can to vary routines at some stage. 26-27th Go with the flow socially, though stick to your own guns at work. OPPORTUNITIES: 22-23rd There are many signposts to the future, as long as you keep your eyes open for them. LIMITING INFLUENCES: 1-2nd Not too much in the way or variety at this time, unless you make it for yourself.

OCTOBER INFLUENCES: 1-2nd Some rather rash statements at the start of the month could easily get you into trouble. 14-15th Out of the ordinary encounters can be turned to your advantage. 27-28th A smile and a cheerful word in the right direction could work wonders in a social and personal sense right now. OPPORTUNITIES: 22-23rd Cut red tape at every opportunity, opting instead for making things happen instantly. LIMITING INFLUENCES: 29-30th Creating the space you need to be yourself is difficult for a day or two.

NOVEMBER INFLUENCES: 1-2nd This would be an ideal time to take a break, even one that you may not have planned in advance. 12-13th Some changes in circumstance should not be expected to work against your best interests. 25-26th Be on your guard when it comes to taking chances with money or investments of any sort. OPPORTUNITIES: 7-8th An especially good interlude for making more of yourself in the social and romantic stakes. LIMITING INFLUENCES: 18-19th If you show a tendency to be judgemental, the situation could backfire on you.

DECEMBER INFLUENCES: 1-2nd The thought of festivities is far from your mind at this time and you are very busy profesionally. 21-22nd Create the right impression in social gatherings and don't hold back when it comes to speaking your mind. 30-31st A good end to the year, even if many of your arrangements turn out to be less than water-tight. OPPORTUNITIES: 15-16th The attitude adopted by your partner or a relative turns very much to your advantage. LIMITING INFLUENCES: 24th Don't judge the remainder of the month on the strength of slight reversals now.

Please name FOULSHAM'S ALMANACK when replying to Advertisers

Your own horoscope by OLD MOORE

The timeless wisdom of Old Moore – now interpreted by computer to give an astounding new wealth of insights and revelations

At last the legendary forecasting skills of Old Moore have been harnessed to the huge analytical power of the computer.

To give you the most complete and precise horoscope ever drawn up.

Packed with exciting new discoveries about the influence of stars and planets on your life.

Based on the Old Moore system of prediction which has proved uniquely accurate for nearly three centuries.

And focused entirely on *You.*

Your own personal birth chart.

Send off the coupon now with your remittance of £15.00.

And enjoy a unique view of your year ahead with Old Moore's Personal Horoscope.

20-page horoscope book – personal to you. Only £15.00 inc. pp

☆ *Most detailed astral reading of its kind.*

☆ *12-month plan of life-rhythms & key dates.*

☆ *Your own lucky numbers, colours, precious stones, etc.*

☆ *In a tradition of accurate forecasting since 1697.*

YOUR DATE WITH DESTINY

UNIQUE GIFT IDEA. SEND THIS COUPON NOW.

Please print your birth details

Date & year _____

Time (if known) _____

Place _____

To: W. Foulsham & Co., 837 Yeovil Road, Slough, Berks SL1 4JH.

I enclose £15.00 inc. p.p. for my Old Moore Personal Horoscope.

NAME _____

ADDRESS _____

JOAN COLLINS

The ubiquitous and perennially youthful Joan Collins' book, *My Secrets,* tells us how she manages to stay so impervious to age. Her horoscope reveals other secrets, like who the *real* Joan Collins is underneath the surface glamour. Collins is a Sun Gemini, born on 23rd May 1933 in London at 7 am BST. Gemini is the sign of the eternal youth, the curious, flirtatious social butterfly who delights in the sheer variety of life's oddities and pleasures. Collins' Gemini individuality gives her mental agility, terrific sociability, a need to communicate, and a dislike of being pinned down for too long. It also bestows cleverness and the ability to learn quickly and live by her wits. The youth or "puer" complex is common with Geminis, and Venus, goddess of love and beauty, in the same sign heightens her charm, playfulness, and dislike of wrinkles and responsiblity. This femme fatale side of her personality is magnified by a square to Neptune, giving her a proneness to fantasy and impractical idealism. Fine for an actress, of course, and she has employed the sultry glamour and sensationalism of Neptune well in her many acting roles. But traditionally Sun-Neptune does not bode well for relationships with men. Mars and Jupiter are conjoined with Neptune, all in the 4th house (early home-life), increasing her hypnotic sexual appeal but exacerbating problems with the opposite sex. Joan has had her share of sadness; her four marriages all ended in divorce and it would seem that a certain amount of disillusionment, beginning with childhoold difficulties, has followed her throughout her life.

But her earthy Taurean Moon gives her an anchor and keeps her going. Underneath her Gemini flippancy there is great determination and loyalty to her goals and to those she loves. She doesn't give up easily, and the longevity of her career has made people take her more seriously. Joan really consolidated her career in the 1980's when she became queen of American soap opera in *Dynasty*. And nothing less than concrete achievement would satisfy the Taurean part of her makeup. Security needs are intensified by the Moon's square to Saturn, an aspect which indicates early childhood loneliness and the demand to grow up fast. It also gives a fairly streamlined, one-pointed ambition which in emotional relationships can seem a bit cold. This is what enables her to play the bitch so well.

Collins' lunar side emphasizes the importance of family in her life and gives her an emotional but cautious approach to life, made even more cautious by the Moon-Saturn square. She has had to deal with emotional hunger and family crisis, and she's been forced into finding her own inner resources to survive. The Moon's trine to Jupiter shows that her fundamental optimism and resilience help her not only to bounce back but also to strengthen her hold on life. Mercury, the cosmic communicator and ruler of her Gemini Sun, is conjunct her Moon, so quite naturally she has become a writer, successfully using the fodder of her personal experiences to reach out to the world. Four 12th house placements show the paradox of the desire for privacy juxtaposed to the chatty Gemini tendency to tell all. Collins' Taurean business savvy has helped her to capitalize on this by developing her enigmatic, provocative image and then writing a book to tell you her secrets. As she says, "The secret of having a personal life is not answering *too* many questions about it."

The cosmic indicators show a fairly changeful period throughout 1995–96 for Joan. Health and work issues are highlighted, as is her changing image in the public eye. A progressed New Moon is opposed by Uranus, indicating dramatic financial upheavals; but Uranus trining her Mercury could mean that she will find increasing success through her writing.

1995 MAIN UNITED KINGDOM FAIRS AND EVENTS

AGRICULTURAL EVENTS

ABERGAVENNY & Border Counties Show — 'Glebelands', Llanwenarth, Abergavenny: *29th July*
AYR Show — Ayr Racecourse: *3rd-4th May*
BAKEWELL Show: *2nd-3rd August*
BINGLEY Show — Myrtle park: *9th August*
BLACK ISLE Show — Mannsfield Muir-of-Ord, Ross-shire: *3rd August*
BORDER UNION Show — Springwood Park, Kelso: *28th-29th July*
BRITISH NATIONAL PLOUGHING Championships — Nyenhead, Wellington, Taunton : *14th-15th October*
BUCKS County Show — Weedon Park, nr Aylesbury: *7th September*
CHATSWORTH Country Fair — Bakewell: *2nd-3rd September*
CHESHIRE County Show — Tabley, nr Knutsford: *20th-21st June*
DENBIGHSHIRE & FLINTSHIRE Agricultural Society Show — Denbigh: *17th August*
DEVON County Show — Westpoint, Clyst St Mary, Exeter: *25th-27th May*
DORCHESTER Agricultural Show — Came Park: *2nd September*
DUMFRIES & LOCKERBIE Show — Park Farm, Dumfries: *5th August*
DURHAM County Agricultural Show — Lambton Park, Chester-le-Street: *15th-16th July*
EAST OF ENGLAND Show — Peterborough: *18th-20th July*
EGHAM Royal Show — Runnymede: *26th-27th August*
ESSEX County Show: Great Leighs, nr Chelmsford: *16th-18th June*
GREAT YORKSHIRE Show — Harrogate: *11th-13th July*
HERTS County Show — Redbourn: *27th-28th May*
HOLKHAM Country Fair — Wells-next-the-Sea, Norfolk: *22nd-23rd July*
KENT County Show — Detling, nr Maidstone: *13th-15th July*
LEICESTERSHIRE County Show — Dishley Grange Farm, Loughborough: *7th-8th May*
LINCOLNSHIRE Show — Grange-de-Lings, Lincoln: *21st-22nd June*
MID-SOMERSET Show — Shepton Mallet: *19th August*
MONMOUTHSHIRE Show — Monmouth: *31st August*
NATIONAL PRIMESTOCK Show — Stafford: *19th-20th November*
NATIONAL SHIRE HORSE Show — Peterborough: *18th March*
NEW FOREST & HAMPSHIRE Show — Brockenhurst: *25th-27th July*
NEWBURY & ROYAL COUNTY OF BERKSHIRE Show — Chievely, Newbury: *16th-17th September*
NORTH SOMERSET Show — Ashton Court, Bristol: *29th May*
NOTTINGHAMSHIRE County Show — Winthorpe, Newark: *5th-6th May*
PEMBROKESHIRE County Show — Withybush, Haverfordwest: *15th-17th August*
ROMSEY SHOW — Broadlands Park: *9th September*

ROYAL BATH & WEST Show — Shepton Mallet: *31st May-3rd June*
ROYAL CORNWALL Show — Wadebridge: *8th-10th June*
ROYAL HIGHLAND Show — Ingliston, Edinburgh: *22nd-25th June (provisional)*
ROYAL LANCASHIRE Show — Astley Park, Chorley: *22nd-24th July*
ROYAL NORFOLK Show — New Costessey, Norwich: *28th-29th June*
ROYAL SHOW — National Agricultural Centre, Stoneleigh Park, Kenilworth: *3rd-6th July*
ROYAL WELSH Show — Llanelwedd, Builth Wells: *24th-27th July*
ROYAL WELSH AGRICULTURAL WINTER Fair — Llanelwedd, Builth Wells: *5th December*
ST HELENS Show — Sherdley Park: *28th-30th July*
SHROPSHIRE & WEST MIDLANDS Show — Shrewsbury: *19th-20th May*
SOUTH OF ENGLAND Show — Ardingley, Haywards Heath: *either 8th-10th or 9th-11th June*
STAFFORDSHIRE County Show — Stafford: *24th-25th May*
SUFFOLK Show — Ipswich: *31st May-1st June*
SURREY County Show — Stoke Park, Guildford: *29th May*
TENDRING HUNDRED Show — Lawford House Park, nr Manningtree: *8th July*
THAME Show: *21st September*
THREE COUNTIES Show — Malvern: *13th-15th June*
TURRIFF Show — The Haughs: *31st July-1st August*
UNITED COUNTIES Show — Nantyci Showground, Carmarthen: *10th-11th August*
WESTMORLAND County Show — Lane Farm, Crooklands: *7th September*
WOKINGHAM & READING Show — Spencer's Wood, nr Reading: *3rd September*

MISCELLANEOUS

ALDEBURGH Festival of Music and the Arts: *9th-25th June*
BADMINTON Horse Trials: *4th-7th May*
BATTLE OF FLOWERS — Jersey: *10th August*
BBC GARDENERS' WORLD LIVE — Nat. Exhibition Centre, Birmingham: *14th-18th June (provisional)*
BBC PROMENADE CONCERTS (Centenary year) — Royal Albert Hall, London: *21st July-16th September*
BEVERLEY FOLK Festival: *16th-18th June*
BIGGIN HILL International Air Fair: *17th-18th June*
BRAEMAR Royal Highland Gathering: *2nd September*
BRASS BANDS Championship — Wembley: *7th-8th October*
BRIGHTON International Festival: *5th-28th May*
BRITISH OPEN BALLROOM AND LATIN AMERICAN DANCE Championships — Winter Gardens, Blackpool: *26th May-2nd June*
BRITISH ROSE Festival — Hampton Court: *5th-9th July*
CHELSEA Flower Show: *23rd-26th May (RHS members only 23rd and 24th) provisional*
COWES WEEK Regatta — IOW: *29th July-5th August*

1995 Main United Kingdom Fairs and Events — continued

CRUFTS DOG Show — Nat. Exhibiton Centre, Birmingham: *16th-19th March*

EDINBURGH International Festival: *13th August-2nd September*

EDINBURGH Tattoo — Edinburgh Castle: *4th-26th August*

FA CUP FINAL — Wembley: *6th May (provisional)*

GOLF — The Open Championship — St Andrews: *20th-23rd July*

HARROGATE GREAT AUTUMN FLOWER Show: *15th-16th September (provisional)*

HAMPTON COURT PALACE FLOWER Show: *5th-9th July (provisional)*

HARROGATE SPRING Show — Valley Gardens: *20th-23rd April*

HENLEY Royal Regatta: *28th June-2nd July*

HOPPINGS Fair — Newcastle upon Tyne: *19th-25th June*

HORSE OF THE YEAR Show — Wembley: *27th September-1st October (provisional)*

HULL Fair: *6th-7th, 9th-14th October*

IDEAL HOME PLUS Exhibition — Earls Court: *16th March-9th April*

LAWN TENNIS Championships — Wimbledon: *26th June-9th July (provisional)*

LLANGOLLEN Int. Musical Eisteddfod: *4th-9th July*

LONDON INTERNATIONAL BOAT SHOW — Earls Court: *5th-15th January (provisional)*

LONDON TO BRIGHTON Veteran Car Run — Hyde Park to Madeira Drive, Brighton: *5th November*

LONDON TO BRIGHTON Historic Commercial Vehicle Run — Crystal Palace to Madeira Drive, Brighton: *7th May*

LONDON MOTOR Show — Earls Court: *19th-29th October*

LONDON PARADE — from Westminster Abbey to Berkeley Square: *1st January*

LORD MAYOR'S Show: *11th November*

MALVERN SPRING GARDENING Show: *5th-7th May*

NOTTINGHAM GOOSE Fair: *5th-7th October*

NOTTING HILL Carnival — Ladbrooke Grove: *27th-28th August*

OLYMPIA INTERNATIONAL SHOWJUMPING Championships: *14th-18th December*

OULD LAMMAS FAIR — Ballycastle: *28th-29th August*

ROCHESTER DICKENS FESTIVAL: *1st-14th June*

ROYAL TOURNAMENT — Earls Court: *11th-29th July*

ROYAL WINDSOR HORSE Show — Home Park, Windsor: *10th-14th May*

SHREWSBURY FLOWER Show: *11th-12th August (provisional)*

SNOOKER, BENSON AND HEDGES MASTERS Tournament — Wembley: *24th-26th January*

TOWN & COUNTRY Festival — Nat. Agricultural Centre, Stoneleigh Park, Kenilworth: *26th-28th August*

Final dates and venues of events listed here are subject to change. Please check with local organiser/tourist board.

BE A SUCCESSFUL WRITER

Make money writing and earn while you learn

The Writing School, founded in 1949, shows you how to write articles, short stories, novels, romances, radio and TV scripts that sell and keep on selling. You simply follow the School's comprehensive home-study courses.

Top professional writers give you individual tuition and also provide personal advice on selling your articles and stories to publishers, who are always on the lookout for exciting new talent.

And you can't lose! If you have not recovered the cost of your tuition by the time you have completed your course, *your fees will be refunded.*

Please write for our FREE book "Writing for Pleasure and Profit" and details of our FREE 15-day trial offer. *No stamp needed.*

FREE CALL 0800 282 468 (24 hour service)

THE WRITING SCHOOL
FREEPOST G15, LONDON N8 0BR

Cassandra Eason

THE usual method of divination with Runes involves casting them. But some systems do link them to months. However, Runes don't predict what's going to happen in a month. Rather the monthly rune reflects an inner cycle of progress and you may find that your own path is different. Be aware of the trends within you and if you feel that a certain rune is relevant trust your inner calendar to harness its energies. You may like to copy your birth rune and carry it with you to remind you of the special qualities you may need to carry out your plans.

January — the key rune is *Rad,* the rune of change that involves effort. Start the year with determination to carry out your plans and keep going, however hard the journey may be. *Rad* warns you that the journey may be hard — but at least it will be exciting.

February — the key rune is *Peorth,* the rune of your unique identity. Being alone is different from being lonely so be prepared to stand out from the crowd to achieve what you believe in.

March — the key rune is *Lagu,* the rune of going with the flow. Be aware of what people mean rather than what they say and use your intuition to sort out the conmen from the sincere people.

April — the key rune is *Eohl,* the rune of wanting something beyond material success and happiness. Look for magic and you'll find it even in the most mundane setting.

May — the key rune is *Odal,* rune of the home and putting practical affairs in order. Make sure you aren't doing all the hard work while others take the glory. You may find it hard to break out of the old routine but it *will* make life easier.

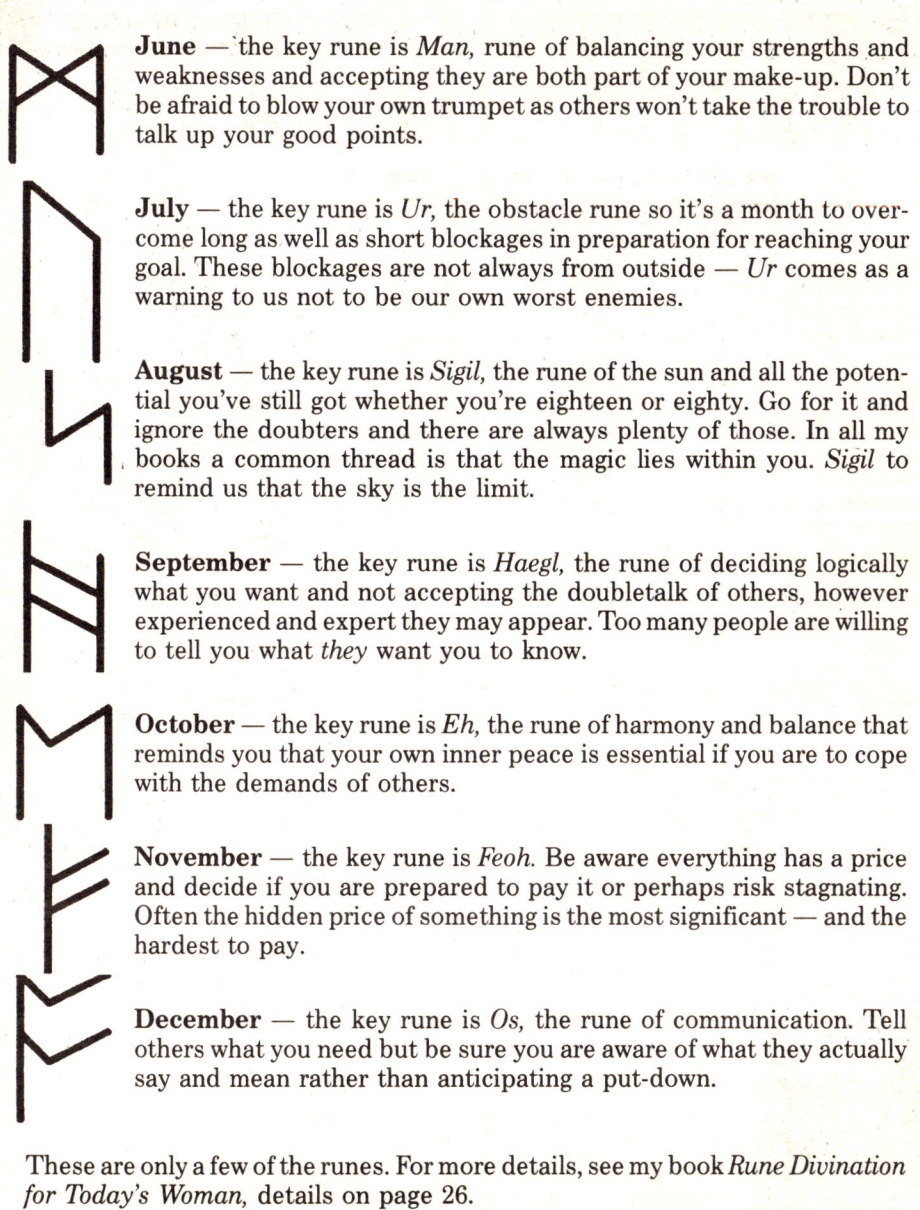

June — the key rune is *Man,* rune of balancing your strengths and weaknesses and accepting they are both part of your make-up. Don't be afraid to blow your own trumpet as others won't take the trouble to talk up your good points.

July — the key rune is *Ur,* the obstacle rune so it's a month to overcome long as well as short blockages in preparation for reaching your goal. These blockages are not always from outside — *Ur* comes as a warning to us not to be our own worst enemies.

August — the key rune is *Sigil,* the rune of the sun and all the potential you've still got whether you're eighteen or eighty. Go for it and ignore the doubters and there are always plenty of those. In all my books a common thread is that the magic lies within you. *Sigil* to remind us that the sky is the limit.

September — the key rune is *Haegl,* the rune of deciding logically what you want and not accepting the doubletalk of others, however experienced and expert they may appear. Too many people are willing to tell you what *they* want you to know.

October — the key rune is *Eh,* the rune of harmony and balance that reminds you that your own inner peace is essential if you are to cope with the demands of others.

November — the key rune is *Feoh.* Be aware everything has a price and decide if you are prepared to pay it or perhaps risk stagnating. Often the hidden price of something is the most significant — and the hardest to pay.

December — the key rune is *Os,* the rune of communication. Tell others what you need but be sure you are aware of what they actually say and mean rather than anticipating a put-down.

These are only a few of the runes. For more details, see my book *Rune Divination for Today's Woman,* details on page 26.

Please name FOULSHAM'S ALMANACK when replying to Advertisers

YOUR OWN PERSONAL
LUCKY NUMBERS
WITH THE

NUMERATOR TALISMAN

Your personal lucky numbers engraved on **REAL SILVER** pendant or keyring fob, computed from your birthdate, and name given at birth. Football Pools - Bingo - Horse Racing - Greyhound Racing - **GET ON THE WINNING LINE** - Job application - Good day to travel - competition entry - **IMPROVE YOUR CHANCES** - Your lucky numbers taken from the "Book of Fortune" could help you to win. Instruction leaflet tells you how. You will not forget your personal numbers, carry them with you always on a **SOLID SILVER** pendant or keyring fob.

MANY GOOD WINS LAST YEAR — WILL IT BE YOUR TURN THIS YEAR
ACT NOW

"Free" 18" silver chain or plated keyring — Please state which you prefer. Send your **FULL** name and address (include maiden name if applicable), date of birth together with a Cheque/P.O. for only £10.00.

"MERMAN" (NM)
1 Doneley Court, Berrycombe Road, Bodmin, Cornwall PL31 2NX

THE SUPER POOLS WINNING PLAN

This top selling treble chance method is the best way of winning dividends ever invented. The plan guarantees to capture every score draw every week for a very modest stake. Highly recommended. Send SAE for full details.

THE CLASSIC HORSE RACING PLAN

Turn your pleasure into profit by using this great horse racing method. Just one horse can be selected at any odds from your daily newspaper. Send SAE for full details of the plan that really wins all year round!

ROBERT HOLWILL (OM)
52 PURLEY BURY AVENUE
PURLEY, SURREY CR8 1JD

☐ **EGYPTIAN PENDULUM POWER**
Let it 'PICK A WINNER' for you.
Allow the pendulum to swing over pools, racing, spot the ball, and competition forms. Time and time again it will stop and point out the winner. Astonishing ancient knowledge and charm power at your fingertips.
☐ **AMERICAN INDIAN LOVE CHARM**
To feel close to Nature, Spirit, and the Creator of the Universe. To bring new friendship and love into your life.
☐ **CRYSTAL OF POWER CHARM**
Cosmic powers encapsulated into crystal form. Vibrating harmony and energies said to make wishes come true. you may use this amazing charm to ask for 3 wishes to be granted.
Free Tarot Reading with every order.
Charms only £5 each. Tick selection.
EDWARD KIND, P.O. BOX 29 SWADLINCOTE, DERBYS, DE11 0GG

CATALOGUE OF PSYCHIC SUPPLIES
MERE MORTAL
• BOOKS • JEWELLERY • PENDULUMS • FIGURINES
• SPELL POUCHES • INCENSES • BURNERS • CANDLES
• CASSETTE TAPES • JOSS STICKS • TAROT • HERBS
& GUMS • TALISMANIC WRITING EQUIPMENT
• CRYSTALS & GEMSTONES • ESSENTIAL OILS
• CRYSTAL BALLS • *AND MUCH MORE*
Trade enquiries welcome.
Send £1 cheque or PO refundable with first order to:
MERE MORTAL
P.O. BOX 372, SHELDON, BIRMINGHAM B26 1EB

Football Pools Forecast for 1995

The following forecasts of teams likely to draw on the dates given is based on planetary indications and teams' colours. No claim for infallibility is made. Readers should use their own judgement, but forecasts can help in the final selection.

January 7th	Newcastle, Sheffield Wednesday, Tottenham, Barnsley.
January 14th	Bournemouth, Bristol City, Everton, Manchester Utd.
January 21st	Bradford, Burnley, Portsmouth, Q.P.R.
January 28th	Nottingham Forest, Liverpool, W.B.A., Grimsby.
February 4th	Blackpool, Burnley, Luton, Tottenham.
February 11th	Chelsea, Chesterfield, Huddersfield, Liverpool.
February 18th	Blackburn, Bury, Bristol City, Bournemouth.
February 25th	Birmingham, Charlton, Chelsea, Fulham.
March 4th	Derby, Sunderland, Plymouth, Q.P.R.
March 11th	Birmingham, Charlton, Fulham, Portsmouth.
March 18th	Arsenal, Stoke, Wolves, Cardiff.
March 25th	Brentford, Southampton, Tottenham, Rotherham.
April 1st	Bradford, Gillingham, Aston Villa, Manchester City.
April 8th	Barnsley, Blackburn, Brentford, West Ham.
April 15th	Millwall, Middlesbrough, Liverpool, Everton.
April 22nd	Bolton Wanderers, Sunderland, Bury, Derby.
April 29th	Bournemouth, Blackpool, Chelsea, Manchester Utd.
May 6th	Halifax, Arsenal, Stoke, Burnley, Sheffield Wed.
August 12th	Fulham, Huddersfield, Chelsea, Blackburn.
August 19th	Blackpool, Burnley, Q.P.R., Tottenham.
August 26th	Everton, Liverpool, Middlesbrough, Newcastle.
September 2nd	Grimsby, Hull, Coventry, Millwall.
September 9th	Newcastle, Blackburn, Burnley, Q.P.R.
September 16th	Sunderland, Chesterfield, W.B.A., Brentford.
September 23rd	Bournemouth, Tottenham, Portsmouth, Bury.
September 30th	Huddersfield, Chelsea, Nottingham Forest, Grimsby.
October 7th	Halifax, Bristol City, Luton, Sheffield Utd.
October 14th	Birmingham, Fulham, Chelsea, Nottingham Forest.
October 21st	Derby, Wolves, Cardiff, Luton.
October 28th	Bradford, Charlton, Fulham, Halifax.
November 4th	Arsenal, Aston Villa, Stoke, Manchester City.
November 11th	Barnsley, Brentford, West Ham, Bradford.
November 18th	Gillingham, Bolton Wanderers, Cardiff, Coventry.
November 25th	Barnsley, Brentford, West Ham, Hull.
December 2nd	Millwall, Everton, Blackburn, Gillingham.
December 9th	Newcastle, Sheffield Wednesday, Barnsley, Brentford.
December 16th	Grimsby, Leeds, W.B.A., Manchester Utd.
December 23rd	Burnley, Sheffield Wednesday, Tottenham, Q.P.R.
December 30th	Liverpool, W.B.A., Leeds, Chesterfield.

The bookies are betting you haven't read this book !

Earn money systematically by adjusting your stake to the odds - as bookies do.

Forget luck. And start depending on logic - with this multi-bet system that gets more than one horse working for you in each race and vastly improves your chance of regular wins. By selective hedging with the right stakes, you can literally plan for profit.

* **Up to six against the field**
  Complete tables of odds and stakes for up to six horses, with profit guaranteed if any of your choices win.

* **Selecting races and runners**
  How to eliminate losers by judging the most favourable events, weights and recent performance indicators.

* **Computer programs for any odds**
  Flash through the complex calculations for any set of prices. Also simplified formula using pocket calculator.

In other words, you're taking a leaf out of the bookies' book by using a methodical routine to slant the odds in your own favour. But be warned. *This system could get you banned from your betting shop. Use more than one.*

The Complete Professional Horse Racing System £8.50

Send Cheque/PO to Globe Book Services, Brunel Rd., Houndmills, Basingstoke, Hants, RG21 2XS. Price includes p&p. Allow 28 days for delivery.

FREE AMULET

Send 4 × 1st class stamps TODAY and you will receive by return of post our highly successful and extremely LUCKY carnelian amulet of the beautiful Angel Raphael absolutely FREE!

Each free amulet is prepared and enpowered by our own experienced Mystic to promote the blessing of good health and attract monetary gains to its owner.

With your free Amulet you will also receive with our compliments, our latest spell-binding **Mystical Catalogue** containing *Divine Magic Squares, Secret Qabalah, Ouija Board, Lucky Numbers for Winning, Power Quartz and much, much more.*

Don't despair, try the world's most potent, beneficial and powerful circumstance and life changing personalised talismans, charms and protective amulets. All fully guaranteed to work where others have failed.

THOUSAND OF SATISFIED CLIENTS WORLDWIDE

Send 4 × 1st class stamps to:

C. O. RAPHAEL (O.M.)
P.O. BOX 30 ST AUSTELL CORNWALL PL25 4UZ

TRIAL READING

For a personal handwritten Astrological Forecast of important events in your life, send date, time (if known) and place of birth

+ **£5** + SAE to:
DIANE CHELLI, B.A.
121 Highters Road, Maypole,
Birmingham B14 4ND POSTAL ONLY

AUTHORS
Let Us Publish Your Book

Most subjects considered including Religion, Biography, Children's Stories, Poems, Fiction and First Books.

AVON BOOKS (OM)
1 Dovedale Studios
465 Battersea Park Road, London SW11 4LR.

RACING WITH THE FLAT RACE & STEEPLECHASE JOCKEYS in 1995

ASTROLOGICAL POINTERS TO POSSIBLE WINNING PERIODS

THE ASTROLOGICALLY COMPILED DATES BELOW ARE PRESENTED TO RACEGOERS IN THE HOPE THAT THEY WILL POINT THE WAY TO SOME SUCCESSFUL WINNING PERIODS DURING THE 1995 RACING SEASON.

The favourable periods of Flat Race Jockeys

K. DARLEY, born 5th August, 1960, should have a very good season. His fortunate dates are: March 14th to 31st (14th to 23rd, 29th to 31st specially recommended), April 1st to 7th (1st to 7th s.r.), 14th to 17th, 20th to 22nd, 29th, May 1st to 3rd, 5th to 8th, 15th to 19th, 22nd to 24th, 27th to 31st (27th to 31st s.r.), June 1st to 17th (1st to 3rd, 6th to 8th, 15th to 17th s.r.), 19th to 30th (20th to 30th s.r.), July 1st to 31st (1st to 5th, 8th to 10th, 14th, 17th to 20th, 24th, 29th s.r.), August 1st to 26th (1st to 10th, 17th to 19th, 23rd to 26th s.r.), 30th, 31st, September 1st to 12th, 18th to 30th (18th to 21st, 23rd, 25th s.r.), November 1st to 10th (4th to 7th s.r.), 16th to 18th.

A. DETTORI, born 15th December, 1970, should have an exceptionally good season. He might become Champion jockey. His fortunate dates are: March 16th to 31st (16th to 21st, 28th, 29th s.r.), April 1st to 29th (3rd, 8th, 21st, 22nd, 24th, 27th s.r.), May 1st to 31st (1st to 6th, 10th, 11th, 16th to 18th, 29th s.r.), June 1st to 3rd, 6th to 16th (9th, 12th, 13th s.r.), 21st to 24th (21st to 24th s.r.), 27th to 30th (29th, 30th s.r.), July 1st to 28th (5th to 7th, 18th to 21st, 24th to 26th s.r.), 31st, August 1st (1st s.r.), 3rd, 4th, 7th to 31st (8th, 9th, 14th to 25th, 28th s.r.), September 1st to 6th (4th to 6th s.r.), 9th, 11th, 16th, 25th to 30th (27th to 29th s.r.), October 1st to 27th (1st to 3rd, 7th, 9th, 18th to 20th, 23rd, 24th s.r.), 30th, November 1st to 10th (1st, 2nd s.r.), 13th, 14th, 18th, 20th (20th s.r.), 21st.

PAT EDDERY, born 18th March, 1952 should be noted on 3 y.o.'s. His fortunate dates are: March 13th to 31st (16th to 18th, 30th, 31st s.r.), April 1st, 15th, 17th, 27th to 29th, May 1st to 5th (1st, 2nd s.r.), 11th to 18th, 31st, June 1st, 2nd, 5th to 30th (13th to 17th s.r.), July 1st to 8th (3rd, 4th s.r.), 11th to 20th, August 2nd to 4th, 10th to 19th (17th s.r.), 29th to 31st, September 1st to 4th (1st, 2nd s.r.), 18th to 23rd, October 3rd to 5th, 12th to 20th, 30th, 31st, November 1st to 6th (2nd to 4th s.r.), 17th, 18th, 22nd to 25th.

A. MUNRO, born 14th January, 1967, should be noted on stallions. His fortunate periods are: March 13th to 21st (17th s.r.), 29th to 31st, April 1st, 11th to 29th (24th, 26th to 29th s.r.), May 8th, 9th, 23rd to 31st, June 2nd, 3rd, 12th to 15th (12th, 13th s.r.), 26th to 30th (27th to 28th s.r.), July 3rd to 8th (6th, 7th s.r.), 18th, 19th, 21st to 29th (22nd s.r.), August 1st to 3rd, 12th to 28th (17th to 19th s.r.), September 5th to 14th, 18th to 20th, 25th to 30th (25th to 30th s.r.), October 2nd, 3rd (2nd, 3rd s.r.), 5th to 7th, 11th to 14th (11th to 14th s.r.), 23rd to 28th (23rd to 27th s.r.), November 2nd to 16th (7th s.r.), 22nd, 23rd (23rd s.r.).

The favourable periods of National Hunt Jockeys

R. DUNWOODY, born 18th January, 1964, will have a very good year. His favourable dates are: January 1st to 31st (12th to 28th s.r.), February 1st to 28th (14th to 21st, 28th s.r.), March 1st to 4th, 7th to 31st (15th to 19th, 29th, 30th s.r.), April 1st to 3rd (1st to 3rd s.r.), 15th to 30th (19th, 29th, 30th s.r.), May 1st to 4th, 9th to 22nd (15th to 20th s.r.), 30th, 31st, August 1st to 16th (1st to 3rd, 8th to 10th s.r.), 26th to 31st, September 2nd to 9th (2nd to 6th s.r.), 17th to 21st, 24th to 30th, October 1st to 7th (1st, 2nd s.r.), 18th to 31st (18th to 22nd s.r.), November 1st to 6th (1st, 2nd s.r.), 18th to 21st, 29th, 30th, December 2nd to 13th (5th, 6th s.r.), 16th to 21st, 30th, 31st (31st s.r.).

A. MAGUIRE, born 29th April, 1971, should be noted on medium weighted geldings. His favourable periods are: January 6th, 7th, 13th to 31st (21st, 30th, 31st s.r.), February 1st, 6th to 10th (7th, 9th s.r.), 13th, 14th, 20th, 21st, 28th, March 1st to 4th, 15th, 16th, 22nd, 23rd, 30th, 31st, April 6th, 7th, 14th to 22nd (15th s.r.), 29th, May 1st, 5th, 8th to 16th, 22nd to 24th, 27th to 31st, August 16th to 18th, 24th to 31st (24th, 25th s.r.), September 1st, 2nd, 9th, 18th to 30th (23rd, 25th, 30th s.r.), October 1st, 2nd (2nd s.r.), 9th to 14th, 17th to 19th, 23rd to 26th (23rd, 24th s.r.), November 1st to 3rd, 8th to 10th, 13th to 27th (16th to 18th, 23rd to 25th s.r.), December 1st, 2nd, 6th to 13th (12th, 13th s.r.), 21st to 23rd.

P. NIVEN, born 7th August, 1964, should have a very good season. His fortunate dates are: January 2nd, 4th to 7th, 16th to 21st, 30th, 31st, February 1st to 28th (4th to 25th s.r.), March 1st to 31st (1st to 3rd, 14th, 15th, 24th, 25th, 27th to 30th s.r.), April 2nd to 29th (8th, 10th, 18th to 22nd s.r.), May 1st to 31st (1st, 3rd to 5th, 13th to 17th, 25th, 26th s.r.), August 1st to 11th (1st to 8th s.r.), 19th, 22nd to 24th (22nd, 23rd s.r.), 31st, September 4th, 6th to 9th (6th to 9th s.r.), 19th to 23rd, 28th to 30th, October 1st to 9th (4th, 5th, 7th s.r.), 17th to 31st (19th, 20th, 23rd, 24th s.r.), November 3rd to 8th, 18th to 27th, December 6th, 9th, 13th to 23rd (18th, 19, 21st to 23rd s.r.), 26th to 31st (30th s.r.).

N. WILLIAMSON, born 16th January, 1969, will have a good season and should win many races. His favourable periods are: January 12th to 19th (12th s.r.), 23rd to 27th, February 7th to 11th, 22nd to 25th, March 6th to 11th (8th s.r.), 17th to 22nd (20th s.r.), 27th to 31st (30th, 31st s.r.), April 1st to 8th (8th s.r.), 11th, 12th, 24th to 29th (24th to 27th s.r.), May 1st, 2nd, 8th to 12th, 19th to 27th, 31st, August 1st to 4th, (1st s.r.), 11th to 14th (14th s.r.), 19th to 30th (25th to 27th s.r.), September 4th to 16th (11th s.r.), 20th to 28th (20th to 22nd s.r.), October 3rd to 7th, 13th, 14th, 24th to 30th (28th to 30th s.r.), November 3rd, 4th, 10th to 18th (14th to 16th s.r.), 25th to 29th (28th, 29th s.r.), December 1st to 14th (11th to 14th s.r.), 23rd to 28th (25th to 28th s.r.).

Please name FOULSHAM'S ALMANACK when replying to Advertisers

Only FULBLOOM helped shape my BUST

"I discovered the leading Bust Beauty treatment. The outstanding way to bust-line improvement." - Mrs. P. N., London

For over 20 years the Fulbloom programme has helped thousands of women, especially with under-developed breasts or sagging or deflated from baby breast feeding or women who just deserve a firmer, more beautiful bust.

NOW IT IS POSSIBLE to have that enchanting bust-line you have always yearned for. Don't deprive yourself of the Fulbloom bust beauty offer that can give you a whole new out-look You must be delighted with the results or your money refunded. **£5.95** + £1.05 p&p for 6 weeks course OR **£12.00** for 12 weeks course sent in plain wrapper. For double benefit, Fulbloom herbal tablets available, same price.

ELDA ORIGINALS, Dept FB/OMA/95
188 Finchley Road,
London NW3 6DR
COD orders 071-794 8288

NEW DYNAMIC MILLIONAIRE TREBLE CHANCE PLAN

How to win First Dividends in first season on English or Australian Pools from usual basic stake. As recommended in National Press. Send SAE for exciting details showing *proof* of clients' actual *wins* this season and how to get a FREE Spot-the-Ball competition winning device and another FREE pools chance in first season plus a FREE "Lucky Pixie" to ensure your success!

NEW UNBELIEVABLE HORSE RACING PLAN

Seven years' results prove claims of up to £100 per week from 25p level stakes plan that really wins — and keeps on winning.

Only one horse selected daily, any odds as recommended in National Press. Use all year round. Unbelievable, but quite true. Your chance to turn the tables on your bookmaker. All our claims are fully checkable. Money refunded if not satisfied.

Send SAE for exciting details and how to get a FREE Lucky Horseshoe-Pixie to ensure your success plus a FREE Dog/Horse staking plan for additional profits!

**Bucks (OM95/HRTC)
Argent Chambers, 18 Coulter Close
Cuffley, Herts EN6 4RR**

MIRACLE CHARM POWER PENS.

Also **FREE Gift of super psychic reading by OCALLABAR**

★ MONEY ★ LUCK ★
★ WILL POWER ★

18K Diamond Cut Gold Plate

Your Name Inscribed Here

☐ ✔ **WIN MONEY FAST POWER PEN.**
Prove it to yourself now. Use it for Pools coupons, Racing, Bingo, Competitions, etc. As you choose winners time and time again, you will see why it's said to be the luckiest Pen in the world.
Your name is inscribed upon the POWER PEN free of charge, so that it works specially for you.

☐ ✔ **INSPIRATION POWER PEN.**
For expressing your deepest feelings, and for poetical love letters, this charmed pen is truly enchanted. No more writers block. Feel the inspiration flow. Your name inscribed free.

☐ ✔ **SUCCESS POWER PEN**
Ambitions, resolutions, promises. Make them come true. Write on slips of paper the things you want to achieve. Then **FEEL THE FORCE HELPING YOU** to control smoking, overeating or lack of resolve. Feel you memory and concentration improve as your confidence grows. Feel the joy as you begin to succeed in the things you want to do. Use for exams, self improvement, and inspiration.
CLARE: 'Playing Bingo, I used my beautiful POWER PEN, and concentrated on the numbers I needed I won enough to **BUY A NEW CAR** and a **SUPER HOLIDAY.'**
PAUL: 'I've no regrets getting my POWER PEN, I've **WON £107,000** so far.
POWER PEN is certainly 'mightier than the sword', for each pen is inscribed with the owners name,then held within an enchanted circle said to be blessed with luck.
With each order **OCALLABAR International psychic ... will prepare a most remarkable reading for you ... free of charge.**
Write your d.o.b. and the name you would like inscribed on the pens. (Paul, David, Clare, Liz) etc.
MIRACLE POWER PENS at only £10 each. Tick selections. Ideal for special gifts.

The names you want inscribed on the pens ....

Visa/Cheque/Cash/PO Card Number .... Exp ....

Name .... Address ....

.... Post Code ....

OCCALLABAR, PO BOX 29 SWADLINCOTE, DERBYSHIRE DE11 0GG.

. .70. .

RACING WITH THE FLAT RACE & STEEPLECHASE TRAINERS in 1995

ASTROLOGICAL POINTERS TO POSSIBLE WINNING PERIODS

THE ASTROLOGICALLY COMPILED DATES BELOW ARE PRESENTED TO RACEGOERS IN THE HOPE THAT THEY WILL POINT THE WAY TO SOME SUCCESSFUL WINNING PERIODS DURING THE 1995 RACING SEASON.

The favourable periods of Flat Race Trainers

J. BERRY, born 7th October, 1937, should have these lucky dates: March 16th to 18th, 27th, April 1st, 3rd, 10th to 30th (10th, 11th, 18th, 25th to 27th s.r.), May 1st to 12th (1st to 4th, 11th, 12th s.r.), 17th to 19th, 26th, 27th, June 1st to 3rd, 12th, 17th, 19th, 27th, 28th, July ⌐rd to 5th, 8th to 31st (12th to 14th, 18th to 21st, 28th, 29th s.r.), August 1st to 30th (3rd to 5th, 14th, 19th, 21st, 28th s.r.), September 4th to 6th, 13th, 14th, 19th to 21st, 28th to 30th, October 3rd to 16th (4th to 6th, 13th, 14th s.r.), 19th to 21st, 28th, 30th, November 3rd, 4th, 13th, 14th, 18th, 20th to 25th (20th s.r.).

H. CECIL, born 11th January, 1943, should have a good season with his 2 y.o.'s. His fortunate dates are: March 13th to 18th (17th s.r.), 22nd to 31st, April 1st to 5th (3rd, 4th s.r.), 7th, 8th, 13th, 14th, 17th to 20th (17th s.r.), 28th, 29th (28th, 29th s.r.), May 1st to 3rd (2nd s.r.), 8th to 11th, 15th to 20th (17th to 19th s.r.), 26th to 30th, June 2nd, 3rd, 5th to 8th (7th, 8th s.r.), 12th to 22nd (17th, 19th to 21st s.r.), 29th, 30th (30th s.r.), July 1st to 5th, 8th, 10th, 14th to 17th (15th, 17th s.r.), 19th to 21st, 24th to 27th, 31st, August 1st to 5th (4th, 5th s.r.), 8th to 11th (9th s.r.), 16th (16th s.r.), 17th, 21st (21st s.r.), 28th to 30th (29th s.r.), September 1st, 2nd (1st, 2nd s.r.), 4th to 6th, 11th to 26th (16th, 19th to 21st, 25th, 26th s.r.), October 2nd to 7th (5th s.r.), 10th to 12th, 16th to 31st (16th to 18th, 20th, 21st, 31st s.r.), November 1st to 17th (1st, 2nd, 4th, 6th, 7th, 9th to 11th s.r.), 20th to 23rd.

P. F. I. COLE, born 11th September, 1941, should score with his 3 y.o.'s. His fortunate dates are: March 13th to 18th, 22nd, 25th to 31st (25th to 31st s.r.), April 1st, 6th, 7th, 11th, 17th, 22nd to 30th (27th to 29th s.r.), May 1st to 29th (9th to 11th, 17th to 19th, 25th to 27th s.r.), June 3rd to 10th, 16th to 21st, 26th, 27th, July 3rd to 15th, 19th to 22nd, 26th to 29th (27th to 29th s.r.), August 3rd to 5th, 8th to 15th, 19th to 31st (21st to 23rd s.r.), September 1st to 5th, 9th, 12th to 15th (13th s.r.), 20th, 23rd, 24th 27th to 30th, October 2nd to 31st (5th to 7th, 14th, 16th, 26th to 28th s.r.), November 2nd to 8th (3rd, 4th, 6th s.r.), 13th, 15th to 18th (18th s.r.), 20th.

R. HANNON, born 30th May, 1945, will have a very good year with his 2 y.o.'s and 3 y.o.'s. His fortunate dates are: March 13th to 31st (13th, 14th, 18th, 24th, 25th s.r.), April 1st to 22nd (3rd, 7th, 8th, 17th to 20th s.r.), May 2nd to 4th (2nd, 3rd s.r.), 10th to 31st (13th to 20th, 26th, 27th s.r.), June 2nd, 3rd, 7th to 22nd (17th to 21st s.r.), 30th, July 1st, 3rd to 5th, 13th to 31st (14th to 21st s.r.), August 1st to 9th (4th to 9th s.r.), 13th to 16th (14th, 15th s.r.), 19th to 21st, 31st, September 1st to 6th (4th, 5th s.r.), 13th to 15th, 19th to 21st, 25th to 27th (25th, 26th s.r.), October 5th to 10th (7th s.r.), 14th to 21st (19th to 21st s.r.), 31st, November 1st to 8th (1st, 4th, 6th s.r.), 13th, 14th, 18th, 20th.

The favourable periods of National Hunt Trainers

D. NICHOLSON, born 19th March, 1939, should have a good season with young geldings and older mares. His fortunate dates are: January 1st to 7th (5th, 6th s.r.), 12th to 14th, 20th, 21st, 27th to 31st, February 4th, 11th, 17th, 18th, 24th to 28th, March 1st to 15th (2nd, 6th to 9th s.r.), 21st to 24th, 28th, 29th, April 3rd to 18th (6th to 15th s.r.), 22nd, 28th, 29th, May 6th to 30th (8th to 13th s.r.), August 7th, 8th, 14th to 31st (28th to 31st s.r.), September 1st to 8th (7th, 8th s.r.), 12th, 15th to 18th, 20th to 23rd, 28th, 30th, October 3rd to 9th (9th s.r.), 16th to 18th, 23rd, 24th, 28th, 31st, November 1st, 3rd, 4th, 7th to 10th, 14th to 18th (15th, 16th s.r.), 22nd, 23rd, 27th to 30th, December 4th, 7th to 9th, 14th to 18th (15th, 16th s.r.), 21st, 22nd, 27th, 28th.

M. C. PIPE, born 29th May, 1945, should score readily with young geldings. His fortunate dates are: January 11th to 31st (16th to 19th s.r.), February 1st to 6th, 9th to 28th (14th to 16th, 27th, 28th s.r.), March 1st to 31st (1st to 3rd, 16th to 18th, 24th, 25th s.r.), April 1st to 24th (1st, 6th, 7th, 17th to 19th s.r.), May 1st to 3rd (1st, 2nd s.r.), 10th to 26th (13th to 20th s.r.), August 1st to 4th, 7th to 11th, 31st, September 1st to 5th (2nd, 4th s.r.), 12th, 13th, 19th to 30th (19th to 30th s.r.), November 1st to 7th (1st to 7th s.r.), 13th, 18th to 21st, 24th, 25th, December 4th, 6th, 7th, 14th to 19th (18th, 19th s.r.), 30th.

N. TWISTON-DAVIES, born 1th May, 1957, is likely to have a very fortunate season. His favourable dates are: January 6th, yth, 13th to 31st (25th, 31st s.r.), February 1st to 28th (2nd to 6th, 8th to 10th s.r.), March 4th to 24th (all s.r.), 28th to 31st (28th to 31st s.r.), April 1st to 29th (1st to 22nd s.r.), May 1st to 31st (8th to 13th, 22nd to 31st s.r.), August 1st, 2nd, 7th to 18th, 21st to 26th, September 1st, 2nd, 11th to 30th (11th to 18th s.r.), October 3rd to 7th, 14th to 31st (11th to 21st s.r.), November 1st to 30th (1st to 18th, 21st to 24th s.r.), December 4th to 13th (6th to 9th s.r.), 18th to 30th (20th to 23rd s.r.).

Please name FOULSHAM'S ALMANACK when replying to Advertisers

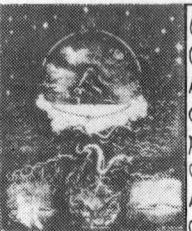

Welcome to World Tree on Root to Kew Gardens

A providence of natural gemstones crystals of beauty and power. Fabulous fossil creatures mighty runes from Wyrdstone ancient ambers, meteorites from space beads, rings, globes and eggs all created out of solid rock

17A Station Parade Kew, Surrey TW9 3PS OPEN 12~6pm RING :- 7 days 081-332-0162

Sky Magick Alchemy Astronomy Know your stars & stones Know your self True maps of constellations Plots of planets & Runic houses £8.88 send birth time INC POST & place to Wyrdstone per birth chart reading

Newly Wrought After 1,000 Years in Darkness

Runic Works With Wondrous Virtues PURE METAL SYMBOLS

Rings crafted for Health, Healing, Inspiration, Love, Wedlock, Good Fortune, Altered States, Protection, Increase, Enchantment, Empowerment, Wisdom. From £10 SAE for details

Your Rune is the Keynote of your Life

Discover yourself with your initial magically wrought in a pure metal Amulet Disk. Send S.A.E for free catalogue

£3.60 for pure tin +£1 p·p
£9.90 for pure silver +£1 p·p
£55 for pure gold

FREE AGATE GEM

(normally £4.00) with all orders from this Ad.

ANCIENT GEMSTONE AMULETS

Wise Ones of old, including Monarchs, Pharoahs, High Priests and Popes, used gemstones to attract beneficial influences:

AGATE for GOOD LUCK
MOONSTONE for LOVE
BLOODSTONE for WEALTH
AMETHYST to calm NERVES

Now is YOUR opportunity to possess one or all of these powerful Amulets. Each one, polished to enhance its primitive beauty is specially chosen and consecrated for YOU by Occulus, the Mystic with over 30 years' experience. **£4 each** post paid, including exclusive carrying purse. Immediate despatch.

ANCIENT MAGICAL TALISMANS

Based upon potent designs, up to 3,000 years old, of the greatest Magicians. All have undergone Occult Consecration and are hand-finished. Many people throughout history have used them to benefit their lives. Now YOU too can possess one or all:

No. 57-THE FAMOUS WISHING POUCH:
"Ask and ye shall receive"
No. 15-for EXAMINATIONS
No. 12-for STUDY & KNOWLEDGE
No. 2-for PROTECTION from EVIL
No. 16-for GAMBLING
No. 4-for MAGIC POWERS
No. 3-for HEALTH

£5.00 each post free. Immediate despatch. With simple instructions and carrying pouch.

TALISMAN OF KING OF SOLOMON

The famous Pentacle diamond hand-engraved in finest hallmarked silver £15.95.

Order NOW and receive free gift of a beautiful Agate gem and free catalogue or . . .
Send four 1st class stamps for latest illustrated 50 page catalogue of superb Pendants, Talismans, Ancient Egyptian Amulets. YOUR NAME in Egyptian hieroglyphics! Miraculous Medallions, fabulous Charms, rare Seals, Magic Rings. The world's largest range in solid Gold and Silver.

OCCULUS (Dept M5), Ra House,
7 The Fairways, Leamington Spa,
CV32 6PU

QUICK HELP

Write to me about YOUR PROBLEMS, and I promise some GOOD ADVICE
I do not promise instant miracles in every case, but where appropriate, I will send POWERFUL TALISMANS and MANTRAS

HELP LINE

I only charge £5 so write to me in detail with your full date of birth or photo

GHOSH
Post Box 13 Portsmouth

ARCHAEOLOGY
PROVES THE BIBLE

Professor Yadin, dean of archaeology in the Hebrew university in Jerusalem, testifies that archaeology is proving the accuracy of biblical history.
Read the Bible's message of hope.

Send for your FREE booklet to:

DAWN BIBLE STUDENTS (OM)
P.O. BOX 136, CHESHAM, BUCKS HP5 3EB

. .72. .

BEST SOWING AND PLANTING TIMES
FOR THE YEAR IN THE YEAR 1995

WHEN TO PLANT OR SOW TO GET THE BEST RESULTS BY THE MOON

PEAS, BEANS, FLOWERING VEGETABLES AND PLANTS WHICH PRODUCE FRUIT ABOVE THE GROUND SHOULD ALWAYS BE SOWN WHEN THE MOON IS GOING TO THE FULL. POTATOES AND ROOT CROPS SHOULD ALWAYS BE SOWN WHEN THE MOON IS LOW AND BELOW THE EARTH. IF YOU SOW, PLANT OR RE-POT AT THE TIMES SET OUT BELOW IT IS REASONABLY CERTAIN YOU WILL HAVE REALLY FINE RESULTS.

The following dates are the most propitious for sowing and planting in 1995.

JANUARY 1, 2 ..... 8.50 to 10.20 a.m. ..... 12.10 to 2.45 p.m.
15, 16 ..... 9.15 to 11.00 a.m. ..... 12.35 to 3.20 p.m.
29, 30 ..... 8.45 to 10.50 a.m. ..... 12.50 to 4.10 p.m.

FEBRUARY 14, 15 ..... 8.30 to 10.40 a.m. ..... 11.30 to 2.30 p.m. ..... 3.35 to 4.20 p.m.
Continue to sow peas, beans, onions, spinach, savoys, lettuce, celery, cauliflowers, carrots, parsnips and radishes. Cut early kidney potatoes for seed and put them in a stove or hotbed in order to start them for planting out.

MARCH 1, 2 ..... 8.20 to 10.10 a.m. ..... 11.45 to 2.20 p.m. ..... 3.55 to 4.50 p.m.
17, 18 ..... 8.30 to 11.10 a.m. ..... 12.30 to 1.15 p.m. ..... 3.10 to 5.10 p.m.
31 ..... 8.50 to 11.35 a.m. ..... 1.20 to 2.40 p.m. ..... 4.25 to 5.50 p.m.
Vegetables should be put into the ground this month. Sow asparagus, celery, cauliflower, broccoli, spinach, onions, carrots, peas, beans, savoy, parsnips, radishes, etc. Plant red cabbage and sea-kale.

APRIL 14, 15 ..... 7.50 to 11.00 a.m. ..... 1.15 to 3.25 p.m. ..... 4.50 to 6.25 p.m.
28, 29 ..... 7.35 to 10.50 a.m. ..... 12.30 to 3.00 p.m. ..... 5.20 to 6.50 p.m.
Plant rhubarb, artichokes, asparagus, sea-kale, Dutch-turnips, German greens and small salading. Earth up peas, tie up lettuce, and in dry weather water seed in bed.

MAY 13, 14 ..... 7.20 to 9.35 a.m. ..... 11.50 to 3.10 p.m. ..... 4.55 to 6.40 p.m.
29, 30 ..... 7.40 to 10.15 a.m. ..... 12.45 to 4.10 p.m. ..... 5.20 to 7.00 p.m.
Sow peas, cucumber, red beet for pickling, and a full crop of kidney beans. Transplant cabbage, winter greens, caulifloer and celery. Hoe and stake peas, water newly-planted crops.

JUNE 13, 14 ..... 7.10 to 9.20 a.m. ..... 11.35 to 2.50 p.m. ..... 6.05 to 8.10 p.m.
28, 29 ..... 7.40 to 10.10 a.m. ..... 12.20 to 3.10 p.m. ..... 5.10 to 7.30 p.m.
Top beans and peas to assist the filling of the pods. Set kidney beans and transplant cabbage, savoy, broccoli and sow turnips. Thin out onions, leeks, parsnips and early turnips.

JULY 12, 13 ..... 7.15 to 9.20 a.m. ..... 12.00 to 2.55 p.m. ..... 6.15 to 8.20 p.m.
26, 27 ..... 7.00 to 9.25 a.m. ..... 1.15 to 3.25 p.m. ..... 7.25 to 9.30 p.m.
Sow turnips, radishes, etc. Plant out broccoli, cauliflowers, savoys, leeks and winter cabbages and earth up celery. Lift full-grown winter onions.

AUGUST 9, 10 ..... 6.50 to 8.45 a.m. ..... 11.25 to 2.35 p.m. ..... 4.30 to 7.10 p.m.
26, 27 ..... 6.30 to 8.20 a.m. ..... 11.05 to 3.40 p.m. ..... 7.15 to 9.20 p.m.
Sow early cabbages and parsley for the succeeding year, also spinach, broccoli and cauliflower to stand the winter, transplant broccoli, savoys and cauliflower.

SEPTEMBER 9, 10 ..... 7.10 to 9.15 a.m. ..... 12.25 to 3.30 p.m. ..... 6.50 to 8.35 p.m.
23, 24 ..... 8.10 to 10.25 a.m. ..... 11.40 to 2.50 p.m. ..... 5.25 to 7.50 p.m.
Plant savoys, broccoli, cauliflowers, leeks, celery, pull onions if tips appear drying. Prick out cabbage.

OCTOBER 7, 8 ..... 8.25 to 10.40 a.m. ..... 12.15 to 2.10 p.m. ..... 4.20 to 5.50 p.m.
24, 25 ..... 8.15 to 9.50 a.m. ..... 12.10 to 2.40 p.m. ..... 3.40 to 4.35 p.m.
Plant some radishes, early cabbages, cauliflowers, mint and tarragon in frames for winter use.

NOVEMBER 6, 7 ..... 9.20 to 11.35 a.m. ..... 1.20 to 3.10 p.m.
21, 22 ..... 9.00 to 10.50 a.m. ..... 12.45 to 2.45 p.m.
Dig in ground where the crops are carried off and which is not intended to plant again till spring. Shallots are readily propagated by offsets.

DECEMBER 6, 7 ..... 9.25 to 11.40 a.m. ..... 1.10 to 2.50 p.m.
21, 22 ..... 9.10 to 11.25 a.m. ..... 12.55 to 2.40 p.m.
Earth up celery. Sow small salad in warm borders, covered with mats.

The above times are Greenwich Mean Time.
Allowances must be made for British Summer Time.

Greyhound Racing Numbers Forecasts

This Trap Numbers Forecast may Point the Way to Possible Success in 1995

In the following forecasts, based on a combination of the numbers ruling the area and of the most prominent fortunate planetary number during the period given, the system is followed of giving each area of the country the most propitious dates for that area and the lucky numbers operative between those dates. The first number should be the winner and the second number should be the second dog, and these numbers are printed in bold type below.

While making no claim to infallibility, the compiler of this feature hopes that the information set out below will prove helpful and beneficial to those readers who enjoy an occasional jaunt to the Greyhound Racing Meetings in the particular area mentioned.

LONDON

Jan.	3/13 **5 4**	Feb.	2/11 **3 6**	Mar.	3/14 **2 1**		
	18/26 **4 1**		15/25 **3 4**		20/29 **6 4**		
Apr.	4/15 **6 1**	May	5/15 **2 4**	June	1/12 **1 3**		
	20/29 **4 6**		22/27 **1 5**		16/27 **2 5**		
July	1/13 **5 1**	Aug.	3/14 **2 3**	Sep.	4/15 **6 3**		
	18/29 **4 5**		18/30 **3 5**		22/30 **5 2**		
Oct.	7/16 **1 6**	Nov.	1/11 **4 2**	Dec.	6/14 **6 5**		
	20/28 **4 3**		21/28 **1 2**		18/27 **5 3**		

BIRMINGHAM

Jan.	6/14 **2 6**	Feb.	4/13 **3 1**	Mar.	6/17 **5 6**		
	20/30 **3 2**		17/28 **6 2**		20/28 **2 4**		
Apr.	1/12 **1 6**	May	4/13 **3 5**	June	3/14 **6 1**		
	15/18 **5 2**		18/29 **2 1**		19/28 **1 2**		
July	4/15 **4 1**	Aug.	2/9 **5 4**	Sep.	1/13 **4 2**		
	20/29 **6 3**		16/28 **5 1**		20/30 **2 6**		
Oct.	5/14 **3 2**	Nov.	6/15 **6 4**	Dec.	2/11 **4 5**		
	19/31 **1 4**		20/28 **4 3**		18/29 **1 5**		

MANCHESTER

Jan.	2/12 **6 2**	Feb.	6/14 **3 4**	Mar.	1/11 **5 6**		
	20/28 **3 1**		17/25 **4 1**		15/25 **4 6**		
Apr.	1/13 **3 6**	May	2/11 **1 3**	June	5/16 **6 5**		
	17/27 **2 3**		15/26 **2 5**		19/28 **5 3**		
July	3/14 **2 1**	Aug.	5/14 **1 4**	Sep.	1/11 **4 2**		
	21/29 **2 6**		19/28 **3 2**		15/26 **6 5**		
Oct.	2/12 **3 1**	Nov.	4/16 **6 4**	Dec.	4/15 **1 2**		
	18/30 **1 6**		20/29 **6 1**		20/30 **5 2**		

NEWCASTLE

Jan.	4/14 **5 3**	Feb.	2/15 **2 3**	Mar.	6/17 **4 6**		
	20/28 **3 4**		19/28 **1 2**		21/28 **5 4**		
Apr.	3/13 **6 2**	May	1/11 **4 3**	June	5/16 **3 5**		
	17/27 **2 4**		18/30 **1 3**		19/30 **2 6**		
July	7/15 **1 5**	Aug.	3/14 **2 5**	Sep.	5/16 **3 6**		
	22/31 **5 6**		18/30 **6 3**		20/30 **4 5**		
Oct.	5/14 **5 1**	Nov.	4/13 **2 3**	Dec.	1/12 **6 5**		
	17/28 **2 5**		17/27 **5 2**		16/27 **1 2**		

SHEFFIELD

Jan.	2/12 **6 3**	Feb.	1/11 **3 4**	Mar.	3/13 **4 2**		
	17/28 **4 3**		15/25 **1 5**		18/27 **6 2**		
Apr.	3/14 **5 4**	May	1/12 **4 1**	June	5/16 **1 3**		
	17/27 **6 4**		19/31 **3 1**		19/28 **5 1**		
July	6/15 **5 6**	Aug.	2/14 **2 4**	Sep.	1/12 **3 2**		
	18/29 **4 5**		17/26 **5 3**		16/26 **2 1**		
Oct.	2/13 **6 1**	Nov.	1/13 **4 6**	Dec.	5/14 **3 5**		
	16/27 **1 4**		17/28 **1 6**		21/30 **3 6**		

WALES

Jan.	5/17 **4 2**	Feb.	6/18 **1 6**	Mar.	2/11 **3 5**		
	21/31 **2 1**		20/27 **6 3**		15/27 **1 4**		
Apr.	1/12 **4 1**	May	5/16 **2 5**	June	1/10 **6 4**		
	18/29 **3 2**		20/29 **1 3**		14/24 **5 2**		
July	1/12 **2 6**	Aug.	3/15 **5 3**	Sep.	4/13 **6 1**		
	20/29 **3 1**		18/30 **4 5**		19/29 **1 2**		
Oct.	4/16 **2 3**	Nov.	6/15 **5 1**	Dec.	4/14 **4 6**		
	20/31 **4 3**		18/29 **1 5**		18/30 **6 2**		

SOUTH OF ENGLAND

Jan.	5/17 **2 4**	Feb.	3/11 **3 4**	Mar.	6/16 **5 4**		
	23/30 **3 6**		15/25 **5 6**		21/31 **6 5**		
Apr.	7/17 **2 1**	May	5/13 **4 3**	June	3/12 **5 2**		
	20/30 **2 3**		19/29 **1 2**		15/26 **6 5**		
July	1/13 **3 4**	Aug.	3/12 **4 5**	Sept.	4/16 **1 4**		
	19/28 **1 6**		17/28 **3 6**		20/30 **4 6**		
Oct.	7/17 **5 1**	Nov.	4/15 **6 4**	Dec.	6/18 **2 5**		
	21/31 **5 6**		20/30 **2 6**		23/31 **3 5**		

BINGO
YOUR LUCKY DATES IN 1995

CAPRICORN (BIRTHDAYS DECEMBER 22nd to JANUARY 20th)—January 1st to March 2nd, April 18th to June 10th, August 10th to September 7th, November 27th to December 21st.

AQUARIUS (BIRTHDAYS JANUARY 21st to FEBRUARY 19th)— January 7th to March 28th, May 3rd to July 11th, August 29th to November 4th, December 22nd to 31st.

PISCES (BIRTHDAYS FEBRUARY 20th to MARCH 20th)—January 1st to 7th, February 19th to April 22nd, June 21st to July 29th, October 11th to November 22nd.

ARIES (BIRTHDAYS MARCH 21st to APRIL 20th)— January 8th to February 19th, March 21st to May 16th, July 23rd to August 23rd, November 3rd to December 12th.

TAURUS (BIRTHDAYS APRIL 21st to MAY 21st)—January 1st to 20th, February 5th to May 21st, August 11th to September 23rd, October 10th to December 31st.

GEMINI (BIRTHDAYS MAY 22nd to JUNE 21st)—January 6th to March 14th, May 2nd to July 10th, August 30th to October 23rd, December 21st to 31st.

CANCER (BIRTHDAYS JUNE 22nd to JULY 22nd)—January 1st to 22nd, February 4th to April 21st, May 17th to July 28th, October 10th to November 23rd.

LEO (BIRTHDAYS JULY 23rd to AUGUST 23rd)—January 7th to February 4th, March 22nd to May 19th, July 24th to August 25th, September 17th to October 10th, November 4th to December 22nd.

VIRGO (BIRTHDAYS AUGUST 24th to SEPTEMBER 23rd)—January 1st to March 2nd, April 17th to July 21st, August 10th to September 16th, November 27th to December 31st.

LIBRA (BIRTHDAYS SEPTEMBER 24th to OCTOBER 23rd)—January 6th to March 28th, April 23rd to May 16th, June 11th to July 5th, July 22nd to September 7th, September 17th to November 4th.

SCORPIO (BIRTHDAYS OCTOBER 24th to NOVEMBER 22nd)— February 21st to April 2nd, May 17th to June 10th, July 6th to July 29th, September 8th to October 20th, November 4th to November 22nd.

SAGITTARIUS (BIRTHDAYS NOVEMER 23rd to DECEMBER 21st)— January 7th to March 28th, April 22nd to May 25th, June 10th to July 10th, July 30th to October 10th, November 2nd to November 30th.

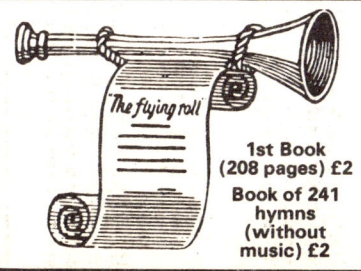

The flying roll

1st Book (208 pages) £2

Book of 241 hymns (without music) £2

TIME IS RUNNING OUT
Current events clearly indicate that it is God's purpose to overthrow the present order, which has nearly run the allotted 6,000 years, to be replaced by the glorious reign of the Lord Jesus. This will bring unimaginable peace and happiness to mankind. Every Truth-seeker should read.

THE FLYING ROLL by J. J. Jezreel
it is a book which will appeal to those who are searching for a fuller life. God's last Message to Man.

A. Vincent, 10 The Fell Way, West Denton Newcastle Upon Tyne NE5 5BY

Please name FOULSHAM'S ALMANACK when replying to Advertisers

YOUR YEAR AHEAD

Day-by-day analysis of 1995 exclusive to your Sun-sign

★ Detailed forecasts, using personalized data – even down to the time of day you were born.

★ Each month analysed for trends in your career, health, luck, money and romance.

★ Full guide to your lucky dates – and how your energy rhythms are influenced by the Moon.

★ Accurate character portrait of your sign with insights into your talents, moods and relationships.

OLD MOORE'S

HOROSCOPE

AND ASTRAL DIARY
1995

Available from WHSmith, Menzies, Dillons, Hammicks, Waterstones, Austicks, Martins and other good bookshops and newsagents, or direct from Globe Book Services Brunel Road, Houndmills, Basingstoke, Hants RG21 2XS, price £3.50 incl. p&p.

Almanack Readers Offer:

Start collecting the worlds most powerful charms right now and you will receive a wonderful FREE ASTROLOGY READING with this order.

☐ ✔ *ARABIAN ABUNDANT FAST MONEY CHARM*

Need a lot of money urgently? Some of the worlds wealthiest people say that the ARABIAN charm made them winners at Lotteries,Pools, Racing, Bingo, Premium Bonds, Spot the Ball, Competitions, Business, etc., It works for them . . . **LET IT WORK FOR YOU.** *Jim. 'Is it magic or belief that makes it work? last month I won £282,000.'*

☐ ✔ *PERSIAN LOVE CHARM*

Poets proclaim that love IS magic. A wonderful enchantment bringing spirits, minds, and bodies together. Alas it can be elusive or one sided. This charms powers are made to seek out a partner, stir the passions, and keep the heart true.

☐ ✔ *PHILIPPINO 3 WISHES GRANTED CHARM*

Generations of experience and expertise went into this amazing charm. It is said that you get only 3 wishes . . . but they are guaranteed to come true. So choose your wishes wisely.
Guaranteed to work or **will refund.** Yes, all charms must work! These unique items are valuable collectors pieces. However . . . you can put them to the test entirely at my risk. If fantastic good fortune and the best good luck in the world does not begin to bless you, then simply return for a full refund. You will still get to keep and enjoy your super *FREE ASTROLOGY READING.*
I accept all the risk . . . there is no risk to you at all . . . **you can only get lucky.**
So start collecting now and you could be enjoying 'ALL THE LUCK IN THE WORLD'
As a special to ALMANACK readers these beautiful Charms are amazingly only £5 each or £15 for all 3 charms.

Cash/cheque/p.o. . . . or o.k. to pay by Visa/Access. Card no. .... Expire date ....

Name .... Address ....

.... Post Code ....

EDWARD KIND, PO BOX 29, SWADLINCOTE, DERBYSHIRE, DE11 0GG

Angler's Guide for 1995

WHEN TO FISH AND THE BEST TIMES
THE TIME CHART THAT BRINGS GOOD RESULTS

JANUARY.-Salmon season opens but high water can be a problem. Cold water makes other freshwater fish lethargic. Larger rivers are best bet, with stillwaters generally unproductive except for pike, which will probably feed best on deadbaits. The chance of big roach on bread, ledgering the best method. Chub will feed on most days, and bream in coloured water. Cod and whiting will provide best sea sport with flounders in harbours. Best days 5th, 6th, 7th (A.M.), 15th, 16th, 24th, 25th.

FEBRUARY.-Snow and frosts make chance of big catches of freshwater fish unlikely, but specimen pike, roach and zander are a possibility. Use smaller baits and smaller hooks for best results. Salmon anglers should be ready for big springers. Cod starting to get more scarce, but fish will be bigger. Still plenty of whiting and some spurdog from boats. Best days 1st (P.M.), 2nd, 3rd (A.M.), 11th, 12th, 13th (A.M.), 20th (P.M.), 21st, 22nd (A.M.), 28th (P.M.).

MARCH.-Sport patchy, but mild days can provide some spectacular catches in freshwater. All species can be caught, even tench and carp. Freshwater season ends in most areas on March 14, with many trout waters opening on the following day. Most trout will be caught in deeper water. Cod and whiting leaving in most areas, but spurdog showing well from boats. Best days 1st, 2nd, 10th (A.M.), 11th, 12th, 19th (P.M.), 20th, 21st (A.M.), 28th, 29th, 30th (A.M.).

APRIL.-Most trout waters open on 1st. Stillwater trouting will be easy with most flies taking fish, but river fish will be more wary. Black bream showing for some boat anglers, but otherwise sport will be mainly with flatfish and dogfish. Wreck anglers can get good hauls of ling and conger. Some good rays from shallower water. Best days 6th (P.M.), 7th, 8th, 9th (A.M.), 16th, 17th, 24th (P.M.), 25th, 26th (A.M.).

MAY.-Warmer weather will start to bring trout up in the water and floating lines will start to pay off on stillwaters. Some bass showing for beach anglers, with crab as best bait, accounting for flatfish and eels too. Good time for plaice on ragworm from harbours. Best days 4th, 5th, 6th (A.M.), 13th (P.M.), 14th, 15th (A.M.), 21st (A.M.), 22nd, 23rd, 24th (A.M.).

JUNE.-Freshwater season opens in most areas on the 16th. Very big carp, tench and bream from stillwaters, along with big catches of chub in streamier parts of rivers. All baits will take fish, though sport may be patchy on first few days. Bass now starting to show in most areas, and mullet moving into harbours. Mackerel starting to show, and first shark will be caught. Crab and worm will take most shore fish, with fish baits productive on boats. Best days 1st, 2nd, 9th (P.M.), 10th, 11th (A.M.), 17th (P.M.), 18th, 19th, 27th (P.M.), 28th, 29th.

JULY.-The best month for freshwater fishing on both rivers and stillwaters. All baits will catch fish. Sweetcorn and other particle baits likely to prove successful for big tench and carp. Fish will be in the flow on most running water. Good catches of most species will be taken, particularly barbel and bream. Evenings will usually be the best time for trout fishing. Sea trout arriving on many rivers. Summer sea fish well in, and mackerel will attract tope and shark. Plenty of bass, and mullet starting to feed in harbours and around piers. Best days 7th, 8th, 9th (A.M.), 15th (P.M.), 16th, 17th (A.M.), 25th (P.M.), 26th, 27th, 28th (A.M.).

AUGUST.-Low water can be a problem in many areas. On running waters, fish areas where there is most flow. Night or late evening fishing may be best after hot days on stillwater. Big barbel catches will be made. Sea fishing at its best, with all summer species being caught on most baits. Chance of very big hauls of pollack, ling and conger from wrecks. Best days 3rd (P.M.), 4th, 5th (A.M.), 11th (P.M.), 12th, 13th, 21st (P.M.), 22nd, 23rd (A.M.), 30th (P.M.), 31st.

SEPTEMBER.-Chance of big barbel, and very big roach and dace hauls on maggot or caster. Stillwaters starting to tail off, but good bream, tench and carp can still be landed. Good time for eels on rivers. Summer sea fish starting to move off, but some good bass still around on sandeel and crab. Early whiting will be caught. Trout fishing now getting harder. Best days 1st (A.M.), 8th, 9th, 10th (A.M.), 17th (P.M.), 18th, 19th, 26th (P.M.), 27th, 28th.

OCTOBER.-Rivers now offer best sport, ith stillwaters generally unproductive. Possibility of good roach, dace and chub catches with caster or maggot as best bait. Float fishing generally best. Chance of big catches of salmon ith extra water. Beaches now producing whiting and occasional cod. Best days 5th (P.M.), 6th, 7th (A.M.), 15th, 16th, 17th (A.M.), 24th (P.M.), 25th, 26th (A.M.).

NOVEMBER.-Rain and colder water will make fishing harder in all areas, though fish will shoal tighter and good chub or bream catches can be made. Feed more lightly for best results and scale down hook and line sizes. Some good pike can be taken. Cod now well in, with lugworm as best bait in most areas. Best days 1st (P.M.), 2nd, 3rd, 11th, 12th, 13th (A.M.), 20th (P.M.), 21st, 22nd (A.M.), 28th (P.M.), 29th, 30th.

DECEMBER.-Although the weather can make fishing uncomfortable, this can still be a good month, though it may be necessary to move around for fish. It will generally be a case of taking a couple from each swim. Chub are a good bet except in coloured water, when bread will take bream. Roach will be less prolific but bigger. The days after storms can bring catches from beaches, where night fishing will generally bring best results. Cod and whiting will be main quarry. Best days 8th (P.M.), 9th, 10th, 18th, 19th, 20th (A.M.), 26th (P.M.), 27th, 28th (A.M.).

Lighting-up Times for 1995

Day	Jan. h. m.	Feb. h. m.	Mar. h. m.	April h. m.	May h. m.	June h. m.	July h. m.	Aug. h. m.	Sept. h. m.	Oct. h. m.	Nov. h. m.	Dec. h. m.
1	16.31	17.19	18.09	20.02	20.52	21.37	21.51	21.19	20.17	19.09	17.04	16.25
2	16.33	17.21	18.11	20.04	20.54	21.38	21.50	21.17	20.15	19.06	17.02	16.25
3	16.34	17.22	18.13	20.06	20.56	21.39	21.50	21.15	20.13	19.04	17.00	16.24
4	16.35	17.24	18.15	20.07	20.57	21.40	21.50	21.14	20.11	19.02	16.59	16.24
5	16.36	17.26	18.16	20.09	20.59	21.41	21.49	21.12	20.08	19.00	16.57	16.23
6	16.37	17.28	18.18	20.11	21.00	21.42	21.48	21.10	20.06	18.57	16.55	16.23
7	16.39	17.30	18.20	20.12	21.02	21.43	21.48	21.08	20.04	18.55	16.54	16.22
8	16.40	17.31	18.21	20.14	21.04	21.44	21.47	21.07	20.01	18.53	16.52	16.22
9	16.41	17.33	18.23	20.16	21.05	21.45	21.47	21.05	19.59	18.51	16.50	16.22
10	16.43	17.35	18.25	20.17	21.07	21.46	21.46	21.03	19.57	18.49	16.49	16.22
11	16.44	17.37	18.27	20.19	21.08	21.46	21.45	21.01	19.55	18.46	16.47	16.21
12	16.46	17.39	18.28	20.21	21.10	21.47	21.44	20.59	19.52	18.44	16.46	16.21
13	16.47	17.41	18.30	20.22	21.12	21.48	21.43	20.57	19.50	18.42	16.44	16.21
14	16.49	17.42	18.32	20.24	21.13	21.48	21.42	20.55	19.48	18.40	16.43	16.21
15	16.50	17.44	18.33	20.26	21.15	21.49	21.41	20.53	19.45	18.38	16.42	16.22
16	16.52	17.46	18.35	20.27	21.16	21.49	21.40	20.51	19.43	18.36	16.40	16.22
17	16.53	17.48	18.37	20.29	21.18	21.50	21.39	20.49	19.41	18.33	16.39	16.22
18	16.55	17.50	18.39	20.31	21.19	21.50	21.38	20.47	19.38	18.31	16.38	16.22
19	16.56	17.51	18.40	20.32	21.21	21.51	21.37	20.45	19.36	18.29	16.36	16.22
20	16.58	17.53	18.42	20.34	21.22	21.51	21.36	20.43	19.34	18.27	16.35	16.23
21	17.00	17.55	18.44	20.36	21.23	21.51	21.35	20.41	19.32	18.25	16.34	16.23
22	17.01	17.57	18. ̄	20.37	21.25	21.51	21.33	20.39	19.29	17.23	16.33	16.24
23	17.03	17.59	18.47	20.39	21.26	21.51	21.32	20.37	19.27	17.21	16.32	16.24
24	17.05	18.00	18.49	20.41	21.28	21.52	21.31	20.35	19.25	17.19	16.31	16.25
25	17.06	18.02	18.50	20.42	21.29	21.52	21.29	20.33	19.22	17.17	16.30	16.26
26	17.08	18.04	19.52	20.44	21.30	21.52	21.28	20.30	19.20	17.15	16.29	16.26
27	17.10	18.06	19.54	20.46	21.31	21.51	21.27	20.28	19.18	17.13	16.28	16.27
28	17.12	18.07	19.55	20.47	21.33	21.51	21.25	20.26	19.15	17.11	16.27	16.28
29	17.13		19.57	20.49	21.34	21.51	21.24	20.24	19.13	17.10	16.27	16.29
30	17.15		19.59	20.51	21.35	21.51	21.22	20.22	19.11	17.08	16.26	16.30
31	17.17		20.00		21.36		21.20	20.19		17.06		16.31

Note: The times above are when *headlamps* on vehicles must be switched on in the evenings. *Front and rear position lamps* must be used between sunset and sunrise. These times are in GMT, except between 01.00 on March 26 and 01.00 on October 22 when they are in BST (1 hour in advance of GMT). They are calculated for London (longitude 0°, latitude N.51° 5').

GARRY PIPER INTERNATIONAL HANDS-ON HEALER

LET ME HELP YOU JUST AS I'VE HELPED SO MANY OTHERS WITH PHYSICAL AND EMOTIONAL PROBLEMS WHICH RANGE FROM CONFIDENCE, NERVOUS DISORDERS, PAIN CONTROL AND OTHER SERIOUS ILLNESSES.

DISTANT HEALING AND HOME VISITS CAN BE ARRANGED.

**THE BELGRAVIA THERAPY CENTRE
12A Eccleston Street,
Belgravia, London SW1W 9LT
Tel: 071-730 4075**

The Company of Astrologers

6 Queen Square, Bloomsbury, London WC1 3AR

Learn traditional theory and modern practice of horoscope interpretation under the guidance of experienced tutors. Correspondence courses, London classes, July Summer School and list of consultant astrologers.

For our prospectus, write or **phone 071 837 4410**

Try a Powerful KARMIC TALISMAN, MANTRA for 30 Days and if satisfied Then and only then send £15

TRY NOW PAY LATER

Please enclose a stamped, self-addressed envelope with one or two pounds to cover the cost of postage, etc., and most importantly your full date of birth or **photograph,** to:

BILTU
P.O. BOX 13, SOUTHSEA, HANTS PO5 4QR

Please name FOULSHAM'S ALMANACK when replying to Advertisers

Cinnamon for luck...
Emeralds for love...
Scented candlelight to protect against the Evil Eye...

You want to harness that loose spiritual energy that you feel around you, and direct it towards creative goals. Now see how the hidden vibrations within certain chosen objects can be brought into harmony with your own concentrated mental power, to achieve miracles of self-renewal, worldly success and lasting inner joy.

Unexplained till now: mystic strands of magic that came together in the voodoo-halls of New Orleans.

South Louisiana has been the warm test-bed of many colourful voodoo traditions whose origins are lost in ancient Africa. They range across candle rituals, talismans, herbs, incense, prayers and chanting. Now, for the first time, these are all explained as part of one coherent branch of applied Magick. Enabling you to reach specific objectives in your life and work.

* *Winning Love*
Small drawstring bag filled with selected charms and placed between altar-candles.

* *Cooling anger*
Simple stuffed doll to concentrate your mind on the person needing help.

* *Health lamp*
Lighting a paraffin lamp filled with healing herbs, accompanied by a prayer to Our Lady of Lourdes.

* *New Year Prosperity*
Evening Prayers around a lighted green candle surrounded by salt, which is then scattered on the doorstep to protect against evil luck through the year.

* *To encourage prophetic dreams*
Anoint with oil containing powdered sandalwood, lavender and frankincense.

Plus many other traditional rituals, recipes and formulas for invoking luck and success for yourself and others in harmony with the hidden forces of nature.

Read this book. And see how to bring about these favourable effects through the use of simple and cheap occult materials - allied to your own meditation and spiritual discipline.

Charms, Spells & Formulas £6.50

Send Cheque/PO to Globe Book Services, Brunel Rd., Houndmills, Basingstoke, Hants, RG21 2XS. Price includes p&p. Allow 28 days for delivery.

A reproduction of the front cover of Dr. Francis
Moore's Original Old Moore's Almanack for 1778
in the possession of W. Foulsham & Co. Ltd. Note
the twopenny duty stamp.   All Almanacks at that
time were subject to this duty.

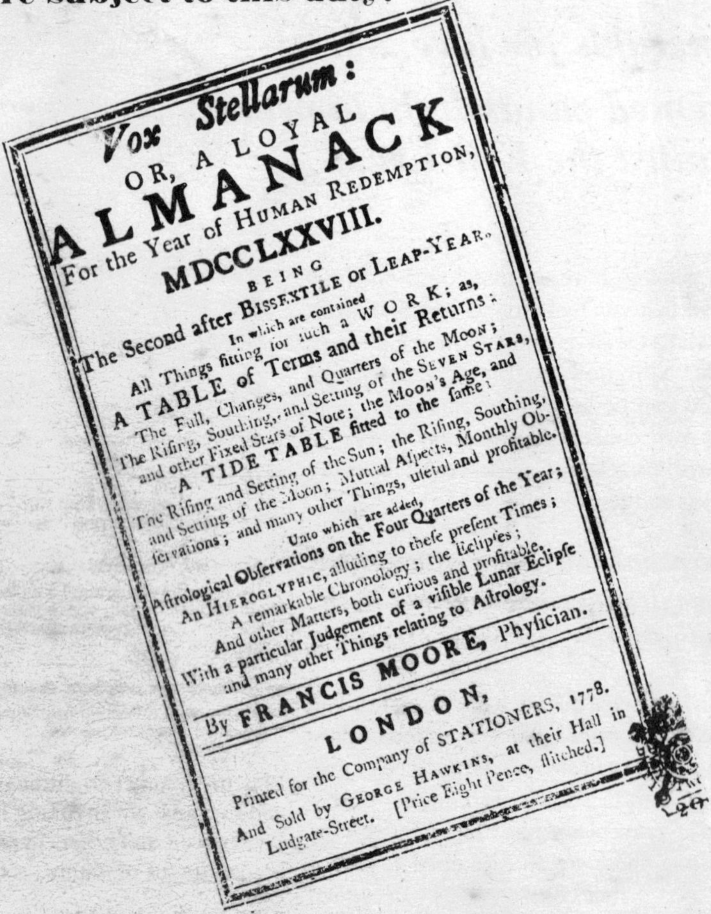

Vox Stellarum:

OR, A LOYAL

ALMANACK

For the Year of HUMAN REDEMPTION,

MDCCLXXVIII.

BEING

The Second after BISSEXTILE or LEAP-YEAR.

All Things fitting for such a WORK; as,

In which are contained

A TABLE of Terms and their Returns:

The Full, Changes, and Quarters of the Moon;

The Rising, Southing, and Setting of the SEVEN STARS,

and other Fixed Stars of Note; the Moon's Age, and

A TIDE TABLE fitted to the same:

The Rising and Setting of the Sun; the Rising, Southing,

and Setting of the Moon; Mutual Aspects, Monthly Ob-

servations; and many other Things, useful and profitable.

Unto which are added,

Astrological Observations on the Four Quarters of the Year;

An HIEROGLYPHIC, alluding to these present Times;

A remarkable Chronology; the Eclipses;

And other Matters, both curious and profitable.

With a particular Judgement of a visible Lunar Eclipse

and many other Things relating to Astrology.

By FRANCIS MOORE, Physician.

LONDON,

Printed for the Company of STATIONERS, 1778.

And Sold by GEORGE HAWKINS, at their Hall in

Ludgate-Street.   [Price Eight Pence, stitched.]

Only the original copyright edition carries this
facsimile on the back cover. Insist on Foulsham's.

ISBN 0-572-02033-3

9 780572 020330